coolcamping
wales

Jonathan Knight

Sophie Dawson, Keith Didcock, Sam Pow, Andy Stothert

The publishers assert their right to use
Cool Camping as a trademark of Punk Publishing Ltd.

Cool Camping: Wales (2nd edition)
First edition published in 2007
This second edition published in the United Kingdom in 2010 by
Punk Publishing Ltd
3 The Yard
Pegasus Place
London
SE11 5SD

www.punkpublishing.co.uk
www.coolcamping.co.uk

A catalogue record of this book is available from the British Library.

ISBN: 978-1-906889-03-6 2nd edition
(ISBN: 978-0-9552036-27 1st edition)

10 9 8 7 6 5 4 3 2

Introduction	5	Brecon Beacons	113
Campsite Locator	8	Monmouthshire	133
Cool Camping Top 5	11	Mid-Wales	139
Campsites at a Glance	12	**Cultural Hotspots**	**146**
Pembrokeshire	17	North-east Wales	181
Ceredigion	53	Snowdonia	185
Luxury Camping	**82**	**Festival Fun**	**216**
Carmarthenshire	93	Llyn Peninsula	237
Gower	101	Acknowledgements	256

introduction

Way back in 2006, when we began to research the first edition of *Cool Camping: Wales*, we knew we were on to a good thing. The generous amount of untouched countryside – and the sheer beauty of it – meant that we were spoilt for choice when finding and selecting beautiful places to pitch. The book was a stunner, the campsites were a hit – our work was done. Cue high-fives and vigorous back-slapping. Maybe a whoop or two.

But then a funny thing happened. People started getting in touch with us. Yes people, real people. They'd seen the book, seen what we were trying to do, and they wanted to set up their own Welsh campsite in the spirit of *Cool Camping*. Or they had some experimental camping pods in Pembrokeshire that they wanted to try out on us. Or they were setting up an organic, wind-powered, eco-yurt camping concept in Ceredigion. Or they were thinking about jacking in their jobs and moving to Wales because they'd seen a campsite for sale and fancied a change of pace.

So whereas we had originally been inspired by the amazing campsites of Wales, it now seemed that our little book was, in turn, inspiring readers to go and set up these places for themselves – to live the dream.

There was a groundswell, a movement – as if the world had suddenly woken up to the idea that Wales was a great place to enjoy camping and an extremely good place to set up a gorgeous campsite. And the world was right. Wales is fab.

But what could we tell you about Wales that you didn't already know? Everyone who knows Wales is familiar with the beauty of the Brecon Beacons, the jagged peak-filled landscape, the limestone caves, rounded hills, rushing rivers and dramatic waterfalls. Everyone knows the Pembrokeshire coast; a soaring, rugged cliffscape bestowed with National Park status and its dramatic 1860-mile coastal footpath.

Who doesn't dream of exploring magnificent Snowdonia and perhaps even climbing Wales's highest mountain? The UK's smallest city, St David's, with its splendid cathedral, the big surf beaches along the Atlantic coastline, the remote valleys and welcoming rural villages – they're all well-known attractions, but until you get out there and experience them for yourself, you can't really appreciate the magic of this remarkable place. And because so much of what makes Wales special is outdoors and countrified, camping is simply the best way to make the most of it and enjoy it all.

So here we are with a second edition and, boy, have we got a lot to share with you. Luxury camping, in particular, has just exploded across Wales, new campsites have opened, old campsites have been taken over – and old friendships have been rekindled as we've been meandering methodically through this western wonderland.

Our five expert authors have visited hundreds of sites, both officially and incognito, to seek out the true gems; pitching up, checking up, weighing up and seeking out. We've added 30 brand-new sites, giving you a choice of 60 exceptional places to pitch your tent – all inspected and approved by our team of expert writers and avid campers.

As usual, we've zoned in on all the essential practical information you'll need, including the 'Nearest Decent Pub' and what to do 'If It Rains'. We've also added full features on luxury camping, the unmissable festivals of Wales and the cultural highlights that will really help you get to grips with the history and heritage of this extraordinary country. In fact, we've gone to great lengths to make this edition the most thoroughly researched, highest-quality guide to camping in Wales.

Perhaps the dedication of the team is best illustrated by long-time *Cool Camping* author Sam. Despite being heavily pregnant, Sam returned to Wales to revisit some sites she'd not managed to get to during her earlier trip, when poor weather had slowed her down.

At one remote campsite, as she was being shown around in a Land Rover over rough terrain, the car hit a particularly big bump and Sam felt something move. Cue a hasty trip home and straight to the maternity ward. Bouncing baby Lucia was born the very next day. And so this book is dedicated to Sam's commitment, to little Lucia – and to all you crazy kids for whom camping is a passion and a pleasure. Enjoy.

Jonathan Knight
Chief Camper, *Cool Camping*

campsite locator

MAP	CAMPSITE	LOCATION	PAGE	MAP	CAMPSITE	LOCATION	PAGE
1	Whitesands Beach	Pembrokeshire	17	32	Strawberry Skys	Mid-Wales	167
2	Rhosson Ganol	Pembrokeshire	21	33	Henstent	Mid-Wales	173
3	Caerfai Farm and Caerfai Bay	Pembrokeshire	27	34	Pistyll Rhaeadr	Mid-Wales	177
4	Trellyn Woodland	Pembrokeshire	31	35	Wern Isaf Farm	North-east Wales	181
5	Ty Parke Farm	Pembrokeshire	37	36	Cae Du	Snowdonia	185
6	Newgale	Pembrokeshire	41	37	Bwlchgwyn Farm	Snowdonia	191
7	Gwaun Vale	Pembrokeshire	45	38	Graig Wen	Snowdonia	197
8	Skrinkle Bay	Pembrokeshire	49	39	Owen Tyddyn Farm	Snowdonia	203
9	fforest	Ceredigion	53	40	Shell Island	Snowdonia	207
10	Ty Gwyn Farm	Ceredigion	59	41	Bwch-yn-uchaf	Snowdonia	213
11	Tipi West	Ceredigion	65	42	Rynys Farm	Snowdonia	221
12	Under the Thatch	Ceredigion	69	43	Tan Aeldroch Farm	Snowdonia	225
13	Outer Bounds	Ceredigion	73	44	Gwern Gôf Isaf Farm	Snowdonia	229
14	The Yurt Farm	Ceredigion	77	45	Llyn Gwynant	Snowdonia	233
15	Tyllwyd	Ceredigion	89	46	Aberafon	Llyn Peninsula	237
16	Rhandirmwyn	Carmarthenshire	93	47	Tir Bach	Llyn Peninsula	241
17	Larkhill Tipis	Carmarthenshire	97	48	Penrallt	Llyn Peninsula	245
18	Hillend	Gower	101	49	Treheli Farm	Llyn Peninsula	249
19	Carreglwyd	Gower	105	50	Mynydd Mawr	Llyn Peninsula	253
20	Three Cliffs Bay	Gower	109	51	Anglesey Tipi and Yurt	Anglesey	84
21	Grawen	Brecon Beacons	113	52	Annwn Valley Yurts	Carmarthenshire	84
22	Pencelli Castle	Brecon Beacons	117	53	Ashera Pottery	Pembrokeshire	84
23	Priory Mill Farm	Brecon Beacons	121	54	The Big Green Tipi	Llyn Peninsula	85
24	Newcourt Farm	Brecon Beacons	125	55	Broome Retreat	Mid-Wales	85
25	Llanthony Priory	Brecon Beacons	129	56	Cledan Valley Tipis	Mid-Wales	85
26	Hidden Valley Yurts	Monmouthshire	133	57	Cosy Under Canvas	Mid-Wales	86
27	Trericket Mill	Mid-Wales	139	58	Flimstone Farm	Pembrokeshire	86
28	New House Farm	Mid-Wales	143	59	Mandinam Shepherd's Hut	Carmarthenshire	86
29	Fforest Fields	Mid-Wales	151	60	Mill Haven Place	Pembrokeshire	87
30	Eco Retreats	Mid-Wales	157	61	Pembrokeshire Tipis	Pembrokeshire	87
31	Gwalia Farm	Mid-Wales	161	62	Tir Bach Farm	Pembrokeshire	87

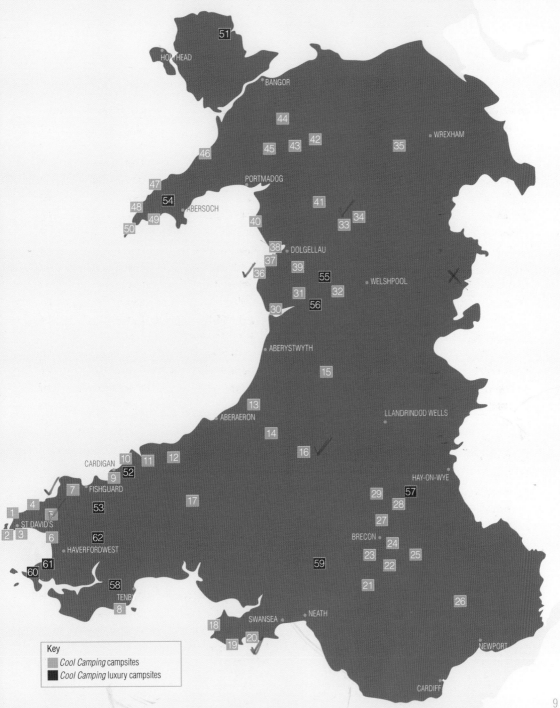

Key
Cool Camping campsites
Cool Camping luxury campsites

1   2

3   4

cool camping top 5

Ladies and gents, this wouldn't be a *Cool Camping* book without us selecting the most remarkable campsites and bigging them up good and proper. These, then, are the very best and all will be awarded a yummy and prestigious *Cool Camping* cake.

1 Trellyn Woodland, Pembrokeshire   p31

Secluded, low-impact camping in beautiful Pembrokeshire woodland. Take your tent or hire a tipi or yurt; either way you'll have plenty of room and plenty of peace and quiet. Pure bliss.

2 Cae Du, Snowdonia   p185

This place gets better with every visit. See the front cover for a taste of the sea views at this corker of a coastal campsite – back-to-nature, away-from-it-all camping with real campfires.

3 Graig Wen, Snowdonia   p197

New owners have improved this site – and it was pretty cracking in the first place. Enjoy rolling fields, estuary views, great cycling and the fizzle and pop of campfires.

4 Aberafon, Llyn Peninsula   p237

Pack your walking boots, canoes and bikes to make the most of this lovely site on the stunning Llyn Peninsula. With sea views, peaks all around and a stream strippling through the site, it's picture-postcard perfect.

5= fforest, Ceredigion   p53

Find the right mix of blissful chilling and outdoor adventure at fforest, where all manner of dwellings (funky domes, bell tents, croglofts) and activities (horse-riding, kayaking, coasteering) combine for a memorable stay and a magical atmosphere.

5= Hidden Valley Yurts, Monmouthshire   p133

Expect a warm welcome at these luxurious, sheep's-wool-lined Mongolian yurts, which are hidden away in a secret valley.

campsites at a glance

COOL FOR CAMPFIRES, PART 1
(OK on the ground)

4 Trellyn Woodland ... 31
5 Ty Parke Farm ... 37
8 Skrinkle Bay ... 49
11 Tipi West ... 65
12 Under the Thatch ... 69
13 Outer Bounds ... 73
14 The Yurt Farm ... 77
17 Larkhill Tipis ... 97
26 Hidden Valley Yurts ... 133
31 Gwalia Farm ... 161
32 Strawberry Skys ... 167
36 Cae Du ... 185
39 Owen Tyddyn Farm ... 203
48 Penrallt ... 245

COOL FOR CAMPFIRES, PART 2
(OK in fire pits, log baskets, drums,
chimeneas, BBQs & specified areas)

9 fforest ... 53
15 Tyllwyd ... 89
18 Hillend ... 101
20 Three Cliffs Bay ... 109
21 Grawen ... 113
23 Priory Mill Farm ... 121
25 Llanthony Priory ... 129
27 Trericket Mill ... 139
28 New House Farm ... 143
29 Fforest Fields ... 151
30 Eco Retreats ... 157
34 Pistyll Rhaeadr ... 177

40 Shell Island ... 207
41 Bwch-yn-uchaf ... 213
43 Tan Aeldroch Farm ... 225
45 Llyn Gwynant ... 233
49 Treheli Farm ... 249
50 Mynydd Mawr ... 253

STUNNING VIEWS

2 Rhosson Ganol ... 21
3 Caerfai Farm and Caerfai Bay ... 27
5 Ty Parke Farm ... 37
10 Ty Gwyn Farm ... 59
15 Tyllwyd ... 89
20 Three Cliffs Bay ... 109
24 Newcourt Farm ... 125
25 Llanthony Priory ... 129
29 Fforest Fields ... 151
34 Pistyll Rhaeadr ... 177
35 Wern Isaf Farm ... 181
36 Cae Du ... 185
37 Bwlchgwyn Farm ... 191
38 Graig Wen ... 197
39 Owen Tyddyn Farm ... 203
40 Shell Island ... 207
41 Bwch-yn-uchaf ... 213
42 Rynys Farm ... 221
44 Gwern Gôf Isaf FarmFarm ... 229
45 Llyn Gwynant ... 233
46 Aberafon ... 237
47 Tir Bach ... 241
48 Penrallt ... 245
50 Mynydd Mawr ... 253

FOR FIRST-TIME CAMPERS

2 Rhosson Ganol ... 21
5 Ty Parke Farm ... 37
7 Gwaun Vale ... 45
9 fforest ... 53
10 Ty Gwyn Farm ... 59
12 Under the Thatch ... 69
14 The Yurt Farm ... 77
16 Rhandirmwyn ... 93
17 Larkhill Tipis ... 97
18 Hillend ... 101
19 Carreglwyd ... 105
20 Three Cliffs Bay ... 109
21 Grawen ... 113
22 Pencelli Castle ... 117
23 Priory Mill Farm ... 121
27 Trericket Mill ... 139
29 Fforest Fields ... 151
30 Eco Retreats ... 157
32 Strawberry Skys ... 167
35 Wern Isaf Farm ... 181
37 Bwlchgwyn Farm ... 191
38 Graig Wen ... 197
42 Rynys Farm ... 221
45 Llyn Gwynant ... 233
46 Aberafon ... 237
48 Penrallt ... 245

A FRIENDLY WELCOME

2 Rhosson Ganol ... 21
4 Trellyn Woodland ... 31
5 Ty Parke Farm ... 37

Please get your firewood from the wood shed in the camping field. Thanks ☺

9 fforest	53	
10 Ty Gwyn Farm	59	
13 Outer Bounds	73	
14 The Yurt Farm	77	
15 Tyllwyd	89	
16 Rhandirmwyn	93	
17 Larkhill Tipis	97	
18 Hillend	101	
21 Grawen	113	
26 Hidden Valley Yurts	133	
29 Fforest Fields	151	
32 Strawberry Skys	167	
36 Cae Du	185	
37 Bwlchgwyn Farm	191	
38 Graig Wen	197	
42 Rynys Farm	221	
45 Llyn Gwynant	233	
46 Aberafon	237	
48 Penrallt	245	

GOOD FOR KIDS

2 Rhosson Ganol	21	
4 Trellyn Woodland	31	
5 Ty Parke Farm	37	
7 Gwaun Vale	45	
9 fforest	53	
10 Ty Gwyn Farm	59	
14 The Yurt Farm	77	
15 Tyllwyd	89	
16 Rhandirmwyn	93	
17 Larkhill Tipis	97	
18 Hillend	101	
19 Carreglwyd	105	
20 Three Cliffs Bay	109	
21 Grawen	113	
22 Pencelli Castle	117	

24 Newcourt Farm	125	
26 Hidden Valley Yurts	133	
29 Fforest Fields	151	
31 Gwalia Farm	161	
37 Bwlchgwyn Farm	191	
38 Graig Wen	197	
40 Shell Island	207	
42 Rynys Farm	221	
45 Llyn Gwynant	233	
46 Aberafon	237	
48 Penrallt	245	

MIDDLE OF NOWHERE

2 Rhosson Ganol	21	
4 Trellyn Woodland	31	
5 Ty Parke Farm	37	
7 Gwaun Vale	45	
10 Ty Gwyn Farm	59	
13 Outer Bounds	73	
14 The Yurt Farm	77	
15 Tyllwyd	89	
25 Llanthony Priory	129	
26 Hidden Valley Yurts	133	
30 Eco Retreats	157	
31 Gwalia Farm	161	
32 Strawberry Skys	167	
34 Pistyll Rhaeadr	177	
36 Cae Du	185	
39 Owen Tyddyn Farm	203	
44 Gwern Gôf Isaf Farm	229	
45 Llyn Gwynant	233	
46 Aberafon	237	
48 Penrallt	245	
49 Treheli Farm	249	
50 Mynydd Mawr	253	

ROMANTIC RETREAT

2 Rhosson Ganol	21	
4 Trellyn Woodland	31	
5 Ty Parke Farm	37	
7 Gwaun Vale	45	
9 fforest	53	
10 Ty Gwyn Farm	59	
11 Tipi West	65	
12 Under the Thatch	69	
13 Outer Bounds	73	
14 The Yurt Farm	77	
15 Tyllwyd	89	
16 Rhandirmwyn	93	
17 Larkhill Tipis	97	
30 Eco Retreats	157	
31 Gwalia Farm	161	
32 Strawberry Skys	167	
38 Graig Wen	197	
45 Llyn Gwynant	233	
46 Aberafon	237	
48 Penrallt	245	

LAKESIDE CHILLING

16 Rhandirmwyn	93	
29 Fforest Fields	151	
41 Bwch-yn-uchaf	213	
45 Llyn Gwynant	233	

RIVERSIDE CHILLING

6 Newgale	41	
12 Under the Thatch	69	
15 Tyllwyd	89	
16 Rhandirmwyn	93	
23 Priory Mill Farm	121	
25 Llanthony Priory (not Court Farm)	129	
27 Trericket Mill	139	

30	Eco Retreats	157
31	Gwalia Farm	161
43	Tan Aeldroch Farm	225
45	Llyn Gwynant	233

BEACH WITHIN REACH

1	Whitesands Beach	17
2	Rhosson Ganol	21
3	Caerfai Farm and Caerfai Bay	27
4	Trellyn Woodland	31
5	Ty Parke Farm	37
6	Newgale	41
8	Skrinkle Bay	49
10	Ty Gwyn Farm	59
11	Tipi West	65
13	Outer Bounds	73
18	Hillend	101
19	Carreglwyd	105
20	Three Cliffs Bay	109
31	Gwalia Farm	161
36	Cae Du	185
37	Bwlchgwyn Farm	191
38	Graig Wen	197
40	Shell Island	207
46	Aberafon	237
47	Tir Bach	241
48	Penrallt	245
50	Mynydd Mawr	253

SURF'S UP

1	Whitesands Beach	17
2	Rhosson Ganol	21
4	Trellyn Woodland	31
5	Ty Parke Farm	37
6	Newgale	41
10	Ty Gwyn Farm	59

18	Hillend	101
37	Bwlchgwyn Farm	191
39	Graig Wen	197
46	Aberafon	237
48	Penrallt	245
49	Treheli Farm	249

WET 'N' WILD

2	Rhosson Ganol	21
5	Ty Parke Farm	37
27	Trericket Mill	139
31	Gwalia Farm	161
37	Bwlchgwyn Farm	191
41	Bwch-yn-uchaf	213
45	Llyn Gwynant	233
46	Aberafon	237

HIGH ON MOUNTAINS

6	Newgale	41
15	Tyllwyd	89
42	Rynys Farm	221
43	Tan Aeldroch Farm	225
45	Llyn Gwynant	233
50	Mynydd Mawr	253

FOREST FUN

9	fforest	53
17	Larkhill Tipis	97
21	Grawen	113
24	Newcourt Farm	125
29	Fforest Fields	151
42	Rynys Farm	221
45	Llyn Gwynant	233
50	Mynydd Mawr	253

WALK THIS WAY

(all sites except 14, 30 and 43)

FOR CAR-LESS CAMPERS

1	Whitesands Beach	17
2	Rhosson Ganol	21
6	Newgale	41
14	The Yurt Farm	77
15	Tyllwyd	89
17	Larkhill Tipis	97
19	Carreglwyd	105
23	Priory Mill Farm	121
37	Bwlchgwyn Farm	191
38	Graig Wen	197
41	Bwch-yn-uchaf	213
44	Gwern Gôf Isaf Farm	229
45	Llyn Gwynant	233
46	Aberafon	237

ON YER BIKE

2	Rhosson Ganol	21
5	Ty Parke Farm	37
9	fforest	53
10	Ty Gwyn Farm	59
15	Tyllwyd	89
16	Rhandirmwyn	93
22	Pencelli Castle	117
23	Priory Mill Farm	121
24	Newcourt Farm	125
25	Llanthony Priory	129
27	Trericket Mill	139
28	New House Farm	143
29	Fforest Fields	151
31	Gwalia Farm	161
35	Wern Isaf Farm	181
37	Bwlchgwyn Farm	191

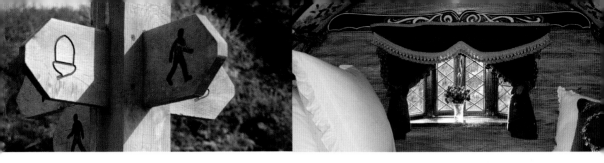

38 Graig Wen	197	
39 Owen Tyddyn Farm	203	
42 Rynys Farm	221	
45 Llyn Gwynant	233	
46 Aberafon	237	
48 Penrallt	245	

SOMETHING DIFFERENT

2 Rhosson Ganol	21
4 Trellyn Woodland	31
5 Ty Parke Farm	37
6 Newgale	41
8 Skrinkle Bay	49
9 fforest	53
11 Tipi West	65
12 Under the Thatch	69
13 Outer Bounds	73
14 The Yurt Farm	77
15 Tyllwyd	89
17 Larkhill Tipis	97
27 Trericket Mill	139
32 Strawberry Skys	167
45 Llyn Gwynant	233

DOG FRIENDLY

(most sites require dogs to be on leads)

3 Caerfai Farm and Caerfai Bay	27
(but not during school holidays)	
7 Gwaun Vale	45
8 Skrinkle Bay	49
9 fforest	53
10 Ty Gwyn Farm	59
12 Under the Thatch	69
15 Tyllwyd	89
16 Rhandirmwyn	93
19 Carreglwyd	105

20 Three Cliffs Bay	109
21 Grawen	113
22 Pencelli Castle	117
(assistance dogs only)	
23 Priory Mill Farm	121
24 Newcourt Farm	125
25 Llanthony Priory	129
27 Trericket Mill	139
28 New House Farm	143
29 Fforest Fields	151
33 Henstent	173
(dogs OK in camper vans and statics but not tents)	
34 Pistyll Rhaeadr	177
35 Wern Isaf Farm	181
36 Cae Du	185
37 Bwlchgwyn Farm	191
38 Graig Wen	197
39 Owen Tyddyn Farm	203
40 Shell Island	207
41 Bwch-yn-uchaf	213
42 Rynys Farm	221
43 Tan Aeldroch Farm	225
45 Llyn Gwynant	233
46 Aberafon	237
47 Tir Bach	241
48 Penrallt	245
49 Treheli Farm	249
50 Mynydd Mawr	253

COOL FOR CAMPER VANS

2 Rhosson Ganol	21
3 Caerfai Farm and Caerfai Bay	27
4 Trellyn Woodland	31
6 Newgale	41
7 Gwaun Vale	45
8 Skrinkle Bay	49

10 Ty Gwyn Farm	59
15 Tyllwyd	89
16 Rhandirmwyn	93
19 Carreglwyd	105
20 Three Cliffs Bay	109
21 Grawen	113
22 Pencelli Castle	117
24 Newcourt Farm	125
25 Llanthony Priory	129
(but no caravans or motorhomes at Court Farm)	
27 Trericket Mill	139
28 New House Farm	143
29 Fforest Fields	151
33 Henstent	173
36 Cae Du	185
39 Owen Tyddyn Farm	203
40 Shell Island	207
41 Bwch-yn-uchaf	213
43 Tan Aeldroch Farm	225
44 Gwern Gôf Isaf Farm	229
45 Llyn Gwynant	233
46 Aberafon	237
47 Tir Bach	241
48 Penrallt	245
49 Treheli Farm	249
50 Mynydd Mawr	253

FISH CLUB

23 Priory Mill Farm	121
24 Newcourt Farm	125
27 Trericket Mill	139
29 Fforest Fields	151
38 Graig Wen	197
40 Shell Island	207
41 Bwch-yn-uchaf	213
49 Treheli Farm	249

whitesands beach

Blink, and you might miss the city of St David's (Ty-ddewi). With a population of around 2,000, this is by far the smallest city in Britain – more of a one-street village with a handful of tea rooms, souvenir shops and restaurants, a flower-filled village square and just one proper pub. What elevates this place to city status is the presence of a cathedral, but if you're driving through at anything exceeding walking pace, you'll probably miss that, too.

With a little persistence, St David's Cathedral can be tracked to a quiet hollow on the western edge of the city, just before it vanishes into a wooded valley. In true understated St David's style, access is via a tiny road squeezing apologetically between a tea room and a souvenir shop. Once through a 13th-century gateway, you'll be knocked sideways by the scale of the structure. For such a modestly populated conurbation, the generous proportions of the cathedral are quite unexpected and totally out of place; an oversized construction of intricate, 12th-century ecclesiastical stone topped by a 40-metre tower.

For such a sleepy little place, the city gets pretty busy in summer when the hoards descend on Whitesands Beach just a few miles to the north-west. This is a renowned Blue Flag beach, consistently lauded as one of the best in Wales, if not in the UK. It's a vast expanse of sand stretching for a mile along some of Pembrokeshire's finest coast, with waves that lure large numbers of surfers. In fact, the surf is better for beginners rather than the more experienced, but that hasn't diminished its popularity.

It's typical of St David's that, for such a hugely popular beach, there's only one way to get to it: a tiny, winding country road that wiggles down to the café and car park. In peak season, when there are way too many cars to wedge into the car park, the road gets blocked and the sputtering queues stretch back almost all the way to St David's. This is why it might be a far, far better idea to stay at the beach itself, where a neat little campsite occupies a prime spot within surfboard-dragging distance of the waves.

Whitesands Beach site is a very low-key place; a runway-shaped strip of land with a shower hut at one end and the beach at the other. There's no reception or any facilities to speak of, but there is a café in the beach car park just a few minutes' walk away. In any case, campers don't come here for the facilities. It's the beach, the sea and the waves that pull in the punters. In fact, the slightly elevated position of the site as it follows the slope of the hill upwards, means that you can survey the waves from your canvas vantage point and when they start to break to your satisfaction, you can grab your board and be in among them within minutes. If you're new to the sport and aren't yet fully kitted out, don't worry – you'll find that you can hire all the bits and pieces you need back in St David's.

As with many of the coastal campsites around these parts, this is indeed a windswept spot, but because it's set back from the beach and is bordered by helpful wind-breaking hedges, you're less likely to get blown away here than on some of the other cliff-top sites.

With all the comings and goings to the beach, it's perhaps not the quietest location, but once the sun starts to dip and the last shuttle bus leaves for St David's, this special place is transformed. With a bright moon ethereally lighting the sea and the gentle wash of waves for a soundtrack, this is 'city' living at its very best. Not to be missed.

THE UPSIDE A spectacular surfside setting and great-value camping.
THE DOWNSIDE Facilities are definitely overdue for an upgrade, but they're not too troublesome.
THE DAMAGE A bargain at just £5 per person. No advance bookings; just turn up.
THE FACILITIES Facilities are fairly grotty and inadequate in peak times.
NEAREST DECENT PUB Nearest pubs are in St David's. Good 'uns include the Farmer's Arms (www.farmersstdavids.co.uk) and cwtch restaurant (01437 720491; www.cwtchrestaurant.co.uk).
IF IT RAINS Don't make excuses, you can still surf in the rain. Book surf lessons and hire boards and wetsuits at Ma Simes Surf Hut (01437 720433; www.masimes.co.uk).
GETTING THERE From St David's, follow the Whitesands signs on the A487.

PUBLIC TRANSPORT Get yourself to St David's then catch the Celtic Coaster shuttle down to Whitesands Beach; every half hour during summer daytime, every hour Mar–Sept.
OPEN Mar–Nov.
IF IT'S FULL Nearby options include Caerfai Farm (p27), Pencarnan Farm (01437 720324; www.pembrokeshire-camping.co.uk) and Pencnwc Farm (01437 720523; www.floronpencnwc.co.uk).

Whitesands Beach, Tan-y-Bryn, Whitesands, St David's, Pembrokeshire SA62 6PS		
	t 01437 721472	1 on the map

rhosson ganol

All manner of weird and wonderful campsites are brought to your attention via *Cool Camping*, with sites majoring in tipis, yurts, environmental campaigns, mountains, beaches, canoeing, surfing, cycling and just about every other odd aspect of human behaviour that can be endured or enjoyed using a tent (or something vaguely similar) as shelter from the elements.

But we all need a little bit of normality in our lives and this includes campsites where us average bods, whether couples or families, can enjoy a standard camping experience – after all not all of us are searching out the weird or eccentric. And normality is where Rhosson Ganol rides to the rescue, and where there isn't a yurt or a tipi to be seen. Neither are the owners on a campaign to save the planet, and there is absolutely nothing strange or uniquely different trying to sell the site to the camping punters. They (the Griffiths family – Henry, Eileen, David and Kate) just want their guests to enjoy their holidays.

But there is something very magical about Rhosson Ganol, and just about everyone who comes here seems to fall under its spell – most are drawn back for repeat visits. Fine summer evenings are the best time to watch the magic going to work on campers,

as everyone seems to just sit and stare into space – or, more accurately, at least the watery space between Ramsey Island and the mainland. A decent view of the sea does this to folk and the view of the briny here is wonderfully unspoilt, with hardly a trace of mankind's activities to dilute the joy.

The wide and unspoilt view may very well be the strongest reason for falling in love with Rhosson Ganol, but there is something else here gnawing at the senses, and it could be that feeling of being in a place where there is nothing that lies beyond. And there really is nothing beyond Rhosson Ganol in Wales, where the lane from St David's comes to an abrupt end at the rocky little cove of Porthstinian.

In effect, this is the Welsh version of Land's End, or John o'Groats, with Rhosson Ganol being the westernmost campsite in Wales. All this can be felt in your bones, too, sitting outside the tent staring happily out to sea on a warm summer evening. Perhaps even more so when the ocean is in a foul mood.

Right, enough notional nonsense, because this is a fantastically practical place to come for that normal camping holiday we promised. Before venturing too far from the site in search of things to see and do

it is worth kicking off the explorations by strolling down to that rocky little cove at Porthstinian, where a few leisurely facts become clear, the first being that a walk along the coastal path from here is eminently possible, with a bus service bringing walkers back to base at the end of the day.

There are also quite a number of boat trips running out of Porthstinian, offering a bewildering variety of aquatic adventures, including contrasts such as a visit to the RSPB reserve on Ramsey Island, to an outrageously mad jet-boat session in the whirlpools and big, big waves that batter this coastline. Then there is the simple fact that Porthstinian is one of the most appealing and charming little places on this coast to just sit and watch the sights of sea and sky. Added to all this is the existence of a nice beach just half a mile away, the city (well, it's a village really) of St David's just over a mile, and the whole of west Pembrokeshire readily accessible from this small campsite, which teeters on the very edge and makes a normal kind of holiday something rather extraordinary.

THE UPSIDE Beautiful and scenic location overlooking Ramsey Sound. Plenty of things to do without driving anywhere and excellent public transport. Extraordinary potential for all those who like walking. The field is colossal so there is usually space if you haven't booked in advance.
THE DOWNSIDE It can get somewhat 'blowy'. No campfires allowed. Facilities are stretched when the site is busy, which is mainly at Bank Holiday weekends.
THE DAMAGE Adults £5.50 per night, children £2.50.
THE FACILITIES Clean, but quite basic, with toilets and showers. Free freezer packs.

NEAREST DECENT PUB The Farmer's Arms in St David's (www.farmersstdavids.co.uk) is the only traditional pub in the area and provides decent food and ale. Morgan's Brasserie in St David's (01437 720508; www.morgans-in-stdavids.co.uk) supplies posh nosh at appropriate prices, and contemporary cuisine can be found at cwtch restaurant (01437 720491; www.cwtchrestaurant.co.uk) in St David's, which features in the Good Food Guide 2009.
IF IT RAINS Get wetter still on one of those jet-boat trips (www.thousandislands.co.uk, www.ramseyislandcruises.co.uk or www.ramseyisland.co.uk). Then there is coasteering, climbing and sea kayaking all within walking distance and run by Tyf Adventure (01437 721611; www.tyf.com).
GETTING THERE From St David's follow the narrow lane by the cathedral towards Porthstinian and Rhosson Ganol is on the left after 1½ miles.
PUBLIC TRANSPORT Excellent bus service from Porthstinian in both directions along the coast from Easter to the end of September
OPEN Easter–end Oct.
IF IT'S FULL Other Cool Camping sites nearby include Caerfai Bay (p27), Ty Parke Farm (p37), Whitesands Beach (p17) and Trellyn Woodland (p31).

Rhosson Ganol, Isaf Farm, St David's, Pembrokeshire SA62 6PY

| | t | 01437 720361 | 2 | on the map |

caerfai farm and caerfai bay

Just before you reach the 'city' of St David's, there's a small turning by the visitor centre. Take this road and follow it as it becomes a single-track country route and you'll end up, a mile or so later, at a small car park that marks the end of the road.

It can't go any further, because the ground suddenly stops at that point, quickly dropping down in a bundle of rocks and heather, splashing into the Bristol Channel with a crash of sea spray and a shriek of circling gulls. It's a good spot for a first lingering look at the beautiful Pembrokeshire Coast, now a designated National Park covering 240 square miles around the south-western shore of Wales.

From here you can see both sides of the coast's character, for just below is the gentle semicircle of Caerfai Bay – a small shingle beach that invites exploration of its rockpools and caves – while off to the right are the cliffs, intimidating and inspiring both in size and in structure.

Handily enough, this is an access point for the Pembrokeshire Coastal Path, the best route for getting up close and personal with the cliffs and bluffs of this wild coastline. And even more useful are the two campsites, one each side of the road.

Caerfai Farm, on the left of the road, and Caerfai Bay on the right are owned and run by different siblings of the same family, but are noticeably divergent in character.

Caerfai Farm is the more relaxed of the two; a traditional tenters' campsite on a working organic farm. Two flat-ish fields look coastwards, but while some tree cover on one side offers shelter from the worst of the weather, it also means that the best views are limited to those camping on the seaward edges. There are adequate washroom facilities here, but what gives this place real appeal is the fantastic farm shop that sells, in addition to a selection of basic camping foods, some outstanding local produce, including matured Caerfai Cheddar, Caerphilly and Caerphilly with leek and garlic, all produced on the farm. No unnecessary food miles here. Morning favourites are the freshly baked bread and croissants, plus delicious organic bacon and sausages, which help to create the most wonderful breakfast aromas emanating from the stoves of hungry campers.

On the other side of the road, Caerfai Bay is a more structured, organised place, where investments have been made in sealed roads, speed bumps and static caravans. The wash-rooms, including plenty of handy family rooms, are of a high standard and spotlessly maintained, but the real selling point is the panoramic view from the two tent fields as folds and headlands of Pembrokeshire's finest cliffs stretch westwards to the setting sun. Just remember that such views come at a price; with a complete absence of shelter, these tent fields are not for the fainthearted.

Being on the edge of Wales, the weather can turn in a moment; glorious sunshine and pancake-flat seas can very quickly be engulfed by howling wind and lashing rain. Empty tents have been known to literally take off, so opt for an aerodynamic structure and double-check your tent pegs.

It's an easy hop back into St David's for all the local attractions, but an appealing alternative is to dispense with roads altogether and make use of the stunning coastal path. From Caerfai, it's a healthy and energetic half-day walk to Whitesands Bay (see p17), perhaps stopping at the scenic inlet of Porthclais, where a tea hut offers simple but welcome refreshments. Regular shuttle buses run from Whitesands to St David's.

Whatever side you prefer at Caerfai, this very special place marks the beginning of the road on a worthwhile journey.

THE UPSIDE Cliff-top camping with magnificent views and tasty croissants.
THE DOWNSIDE Too many static caravans at the Caerfai Bay campsite.
THE DAMAGE Tents £12.50–14.50 for 2 adults plus car, plus £4.50/£3 per adult/child at the Bay. Prices at the Farm are £6/£3 per adult/child. Tents and motorhomes only at the Farm; caravans accepted at the Bay.
THE FACILITIES Both sites have hot showers, dishwashing rooms and laundry facilities. Caerfai Bay has family rooms and baby-changing facilities. The farm shop at Caerfai Farm is open to all.
NEAREST DECENT PUB Just under a mile away, back near the visitor centre, is the Grove Hotel (01437 720341;www.grovestdavids.co.uk), a regency house with an atmosphere-less restaurant (only open Fri/Sat night), but a livelier snug bar that serves decent food. Also in town is the lovely cwtch (01437 720491; www. cwtchrestaurant.co.uk), serving simple, traditional dishes with a contemporary twist in cosy, relaxed surroundings. There's also a small bar upstairs.
IF IT RAINS Even if it's raining at the coast, it might be dry inland, so keep an ear out for the local forecast. Otherwise, head to St David's for the cathedral, a couple of galleries and shopping.
GETTING THERE From Haverfordwest, take the A487 to St David's. Look out for the visitor centre on the left when approaching St David's and take the left just before it. After about ¾ mile, look out for the signs for Caerfai Farm on the left or continue all the way to the end for Caerfai Bay, on the right.
PUBLIC TRANSPORT Buses run from Haverfordwest to St David's (service 411), but it's quite a walk from town if you've lots of gear.
OPEN Caerfai Farm Easter–Sept; Caerfai Bay Mar–Nov.
IF IT'S FULL Glan-y-Mor campsite (www.glan-y-mor.co.uk) is a simple tenters' campsite on the same road, but without the views.

Caerfai Farm, St David's, Pembrokeshire SA62 6QD	t	01437 720548	w	www.caerfai.co.uk	
Caerfai Bay, St David's, Pembrokeshire SA62 6QT	t	01437 720274	w	www.caerfaibay.co.uk	3 on the map

trellyn woodland

There's a spot at Trellyn – standing on the rickety wooden bridge, looking upstream as water fizzles and licks at the flow-smoothed stones below – where the woodland canopy overhead is so thick with branches and leaves that, even on the brightest days, the sunlight struggles to find a way in.

The dappled yellow that does trick its way through the trees lights the woodland with a mystical hue, sprinkling special magic about the place. You might expect fairies or elves to peek out from behind a tree, do a little dance and disappear again. And although on our last visit we didn't actually see any, it's impossible to rule it out completely.

Trellyn is a magical place. It's calm and remote; a hidden woodland playground, where bumping into other campers is almost as unlikely as bumping into fairies or elves. And it's all down to two things – space and trees. Lots of space and lots of trees. Across 16 acres of beautiful Pembrokshire woodland, Trellyn stretches to just five camping pitches, a couple of yurts and a couple of tipis. That's it. So per pitch that's, like, a lot of room and a lot of trees.

Even calling these 'pitches' is a gross misrepresentation. They're clearings, pockets of solitude carved out of the woodland and furnished with a picnic table, campfire area and full field kitchen. A field kitchen, for those of you that don't know, is a canvas lean-to equipped with gas stove, cooking apparatus, drinking water and all the other paraphernalia required to cook. It's also a stroke of genius, allowing you to cook outside in all weathers and to be creative with your camping meals instead of huddling over a tin of baked beans on a gas burner in your tent.

As if all that's not enough to make Trellyn one of the best places to camp on the planet, there's also the fact that, when you arrive, you'll have a basket of pre-cut wood and kindling all ready and waiting for you and – even better – when that runs out, you're free to grab the axe and raid the woodshed, chopping down the big old logs and pretending you're Ray Mears. You just wouldn't get that at Center Parcs.

For those camping in the tipis and yurts, raised wooden floors have been built, providing a more comfortable experience, and comfortable beds and futons are also provided. Rugs, cushions and sheepskins add to the homely ambiance, but unlike other more authentic (and smoky) tipi experiences, there is no internal log fire. A wood-burning stove is provided in the

yurts for warmth and general cosiness, while tipi-dwellers have the outside campfire and field-kitchen options.

The almost-coastal location of Trellyn means it's a perfect base to explore the attractions of Pembrokeshire. Numerous beaches are just a short drive away and Abercastle Beach, with its low-tide sand and rockpools, is 100 metres from the campsite. Fresh crab and lobster are landed at Abercastle harbour every Sunday and can be purchased from the quayside; the perfect boil-in-the-pan starter to any campfire meal and a great way to eat local. And while there is plenty to do in

the area, the best evening is to be had back around the campfire, in your own special, hand-crafted camping clearing.

When *Cool Camping* first discovered this place in 2006, we wrote about how refreshing it was to find such a steadfastly uncommercial campsite and how rare such beautiful, chilled-out woodland sites are to find. Since then, we've visited hundreds of other campsites and covered just about every inch of Wales hoping to find an equal to the Trellyn experience. We've failed. Trellyn wins. And very good luck to them.

THE UPSIDE Woodland, fires, space, trees and owners who care.
THE DOWNSIDE Too few pitches to cope with demand – and too few campsites like this around.
THE DAMAGE Weekly bookings only. Camping from £189 per week; tipis from £385 per week; yurt from £495 per week. Campers must also be members of the Camping and Caravanning Club; non-members can join onsite for £36.
THE FACILITIES Picnic tables, campfire grates, solar-heated showers, washing-up facilities, toilets. Electric hook-ups available. Bedding supplied in the yurt, but not the tipis. No shop onsite, although home-grown vegetables and locally caught fish are sometimes available;

2 small shops and a post office within 2 miles of the campsite. The nearest shop with camping supplies is in St David's.
NEAREST DECENT PUB There's a nice little pub (the Sloop Inn, 01348 831449; www.sloop.co.uk) as well as an award-winning seafood restaurant (the Shed, 01348 831518; www.theshedporthgain.co.uk) just along the coast at Porthgain. There are also 2 local pubs within 3 miles, both of which can be reached on the Strumble Shuttle bus service from the campsite.
IF IT RAINS The miniature city of St David's (see p17) is an easy drive.
GETTING THERE From the A40 at Letterston between Haverfordwest and Fishguard, take the

B4331 opposite the fish-and-chip shop and follow for 4 miles. At the A487 crossroads, go straight across to Mathry; just after the Farmer's Arms, turn right (signposted Abercastle) and, after nearly 2 miles, look for a sign/entrance on the left.
PUBLIC TRANSPORT The Strumble Shuttle bus service (www.pembrokeshiregreenways.co.uk) stops at the campsite as it runs between Fishguard and St David's.
OPEN End May–early Sept (yurts stay open until end Sept).
IF IT'S FULL This sort of quiet, perfectly formed campsite is a rare breed. For a similar woodland tipi experience, try Larkhill Tipis (p97); Outer Bounds (p73) has a similar vibe.

Trellyn Woodland, Abercastle, Haverfordwest, Pembrokeshire SA62 5HJ

t 01348 837762 | w www.trellyn.co.uk | 4 on the map

ty parke farm

British campsites tend to go back a few years, with many having been there since leisure-for-its-own-sake became a normal thing for most people. Many sites have evolved from 'a couple of tents on a spare piece of farmer's land' into their present-day splendour. But not Ty Parke, which first opened its gates a mere three years ago.

After deciding they liked the idea of opening a campsite on their farm in the western wilds of Pembrokeshire, Gary and Annie Loch thought long and hard about what kind of campsite they would wish to stay on. They realised they now had a golden opportunity to create something perfect. That they have been so successful in such a short time confirms that the original ideas were right for the sort of folk they hoped to attract.

Firstly, they were determined to create space for campers to breathe, both spiritually and physically, as an escape from the intense urban lifestyle most of us have to lead. And even though this was a brand-new site, the experience had to reflect the original essence of camping – being more directly involved with the natural world. The impression you get is that Gary and Annie, possibly without realising it, have delved even deeper into our camping past and are encouraging campers to feel just a little of what our

prehistoric forebears must have felt when they were gathered around the fire at night: gazing into the mysterious flames; hearing the eerie sounds of the night and the other creatures out there sharing their lives, but keeping their distance. Although this place includes a sparkling toilet block, with family bathrooms, of course, and plenty of hot water for washing up the wine glasses. There is even an electric kettle in the amenities block. And free eggs when the hens oblige.

The effort to create this natural, but comfortable, camping experience has resulted in Ty Parke having just 10 pitches in a space where 100 might take up residence on other campsites, and the provision of those 'sounds of the night' (very authentic they are, too) comes from their adjacent five-acre nature trail, where badgers and foxes warily wander. Three thousand trees have been planted since 2007, and the young forest is already laying down a soft edge to the wild, open countryside, which is more familiar in north and west Pembrokeshire.

The intention is that the entire energy needs of the farm and campsite, plus all its effluence and by-products, will be produced and recycled right here, with measures such as coppicing, rainwater-harvesting (it does rain occasionally), solar heating (yep, they get sunshine, too) and compost toilets all helping to produce eco-friendly tourism. And there aren't many rules here, either, or at least no annoying notices. Again it is all about letting folk breathe, slow down and ponder. Or stare into the completely unpolluted night sky, where humankind's insignificance is confirmed so completely.

Ty Parke also offers a tipi for campers who wish to try something even more authentic – or decadent, depending on how you view these things. Eventually, though, peaceful as it may be at Ty Parke, thoughts must

turn to the outside world and the Lochs are urging guests to bring their bikes with them and discover that there is enough entertainment to keep the family busy for the full week within an hour's bike ride. There are glorious beaches, quaint little harbours, adrenaline-inducing boat trips, coasteering, pony-trekking, big waves and even a cathedral; and all within reach on your push iron.

Ty Parke is camping as it used to be, with the wilds pushing in around the edges, but without the hardships.

THE UPSIDE Immaculate facilities, peaceful rural location and the feeling of space, which the limited number of pitches provides. Well-organised campfires and supplies. Campers trusted and treated as sensible people. Free eggs.
THE DOWNSIDE Perhaps a little too far from the beach for some and maybe too peaceful and civilised for others.
THE DAMAGE £20 per night for a tent and 2 adults; additional adults (over 14 years) £7.50; children £5; firewood £2.50 per basket, but your first basket is free. Tipi hire is £395 per week.
THE FACILITIES Immaculate family-type wash-rooms with toilets and free showers, laundry, refrigerator and electric kettle.

NEAREST DECENT PUB Farmer's Arms at Mathry (01348 831284; www.farmersarmsmathry. co.uk) is a village local and serves good food. Perhaps best is the Sloop Inn at Porthgain (01348 831449; www.sloop.co.uk), which overlooks the small harbour in the village.
IF IT RAINS There are castles at Pembroke, Carew, Manorbier, Cilgerran, Haverfordwest, and Picton – all worth exploring – plus St David's Cathedral. Why not get even more wet, if it rains, with surfing nearby and adrenaline-rush boat rides from Porthstinian or boat trips to Ramsey Island (www.venturejet.com)? Coasteering trips can be organised by www.preseliventure.co.uk and, if the kids are clamouring for adventure, take them to

Oakwood Theme Park (01834 891376; www.oakwoodthemepark.co.uk).
GETTING THERE From Haverfordwest follow B4330 towards Croesgoch for 10 miles and Ty Parke is on the right, or from Goodwick follow the A487 for 10 miles to Croesgoch. Turn left on to the B4330 towards Haverfordwest and the campsite is 4 miles down the road on the left.
PUBLIC TRANSPORT None, you're on your own from the main Goodwick–St David's road.
OPEN Easter–mid Sept.
IF IT'S FULL Other *Cool Camping* sites nearby are Trellyn Woodland (p31), Rhosson Ganol (p21), Whitesands Beach (p17) and Caerfai Bay (p27).

Ty Parke Farm, Llanreithan, St David's, Pembrokeshire SA62 5LG

| | | t | 01348 837384 | w | www.typarke.co.uk | 5 | on the map |

Please get your firewood from the wood shed in the camping field. Thanks ☺

newgale

It's impossible to ever get completely weary of the Pembrokeshire Coast. Whichever way you look you'll find spectacular views, weathered cliffs and sandy beaches – all luring you to explore them. Nearby ancient towns and villages have their own quirky characters just waiting for you to discover them, too. If you're wedded to your wheels, the coast is a perfect spot for a driving holiday, with plenty of stopping-off points – and campsites – along your merry way.

Driving north-west along the stretch of road from Haverfordwest (Hwlffordd) to St David's on a summer's day, your view from the car is mostly hidden by hedges and hills, until you crest the hill just shy of Newgale (Pen Y Cwm), when the expansive view is so sudden and so stunning that a driver has to concentrate hard to keep focused on the road. The way takes a steep dive downwards to Newgale Beach, beyond which the blue sea looks too warm and inviting to be true. Surfers, windsurfers and kite-surfers dot the bright water, while families spread out on the sand. With the coastline's cliffs providing a dramatic backdrop, it's the very picture of summer bliss. And just when you thought that it couldn't possibly get any better, you realise that a large field right next to the beach is, in fact, an extremely well-appointed campsite.

For beach-lovers, surfers, swimmers, windsurfers and kite-surfers, Newgale campsite is better than any Ritz or Raffles. With the beach a mere 30-second stroll away, the location is pure heaven on a hot sunny day. Most of the water-sporters using this beach are experienced and self-equipped, but if you're new and just fancy a go, you can get virtually everything you need from the Newsurf Beach Shop next to the site. They'll fix you up with surfboards and bodyboards to buy or hire and can arrange for you to have surfing lessons, too. They can also tell you about kite-surfing lessons run from Newgale Beach. With its long, flat sands, easy access and windy conditions, this could yet become the kite-surfing capital of Wales.

The action continues along the coast. In either direction, there's great walking along the Pembrokeshire Coastal Path. Heading northwards will bring you to the town of Solva, with its pubs and restaurants, and then on to Caerfai Bay (see p27) and St David's. A walk southwards takes you to the 'havens': the shingle cove of Nolton Haven, the brash and over-holidayed Broad Haven and the picturesque fishing village of Little Haven. It's also possible to go horse-riding on the beach at Nolton Haven and occasionally at Newgale Beach itself – an alternative and exhilarating way to splash through the surf. Nolton Stables (01437 710360; www.noltonstables.com) can organise this, along with a range of other coastal rides through this memorably scenic part of the country.

Although the campsite has a great beachside location, it's fairly un-noteworthy in most other respects. It's a largely flat, virtually treeless field with little in the way of interesting features. On one side a low bank separates it from the adjoining A487, from where there's a pretty constant hum of traffic noise. It's best not to camp next to the road, unless you're desperate to have one of the spots nearest to the beach.

But when the weather's fine and you can see the sea shimmering from your pitch, it's that proximity to the golden delights of the Pembrokeshire Coast that sees people coming back for more, year after year.

THE UPSIDE Camping next to a sandy water-sports Mecca.

THE DOWNSIDE There's a minor road between the campsite and the beach.

THE DAMAGE Just £5 per person per night; no advance bookings accepted.

THE FACILITIES A new, upmarket facilities block 'the kind you see at service stations' has 10 toilets and 8 showers, with cold showers for wetsuits behind it; the dishwashing room is open 8am–8pm; no laundry facilities; the Newsurf Beach Shop next door sells essentials.

NEAREST DECENT PUB The Duke Of Edinburgh pub is right next door to the campsite; the terrace gets packed out on sunny days, but unfortunately it's totally bereft of atmosphere inside. Better pubs can be found at St David's (see p24; p28) and Little Haven.

IF IT RAINS Rain is the perfect excuse to get in the water, so get some surfing lessons from Newsurf (01437 721398; www.newsurf.co.uk) from £35 for 3 hours. If you want to stay dry, St David's is a short drive away.

GETTING THERE From Haverfordwest, take the A487 west for 8 miles towards St David's; watch out for the beach (you can't miss it) and the campsite is on the right.

PUBLIC TRANSPORT Trains run frequently to Haverfordwest, from where the regular St David's bus stops at Newgale.

OPEN Easter–Sept.

IF IT'S FULL There are plenty of other sites around here, including those around Little Haven and the Caerfais (p27).

Newgale, Wood Farm, Newgale, Haverfordwest, Pembrokeshire SA62 6AR

| | t | 01437 710253 | w | www.newgalecampingsite.co.uk | 6 | on the map |

gwaun vale

Think of Pembrokeshire and you think of the coastline. And rightly so. Perhaps the least trodden-upon section of the Pembrokeshire Coastal Path is that wild and windswept area in the north, between Cardigan (Aberteifi) and Fishguard (Abergwaun). The cliffs are rougher and higher up here than their softer southern siblings, and around Newport (Trefdraith) you can't help but notice that some quite lofty hills come down to the sea to dip their toes in the surf.

These rounded mounds are the rather grandly named Preseli Hills, and the main valley that cuts its way into their very heart is carved out by the Gwaun river. Buried in its green folds is the Gwaun Vale Touring Park. The site lies on steep, terraced ground facing north-east, with a magnificent view of the Preseli Hills and just a glimpse of the sea from the very top of the site.

It seems odd, but somehow satisfying, that a campsite in Pembrokeshire can have its roots so thoroughly in the hills rather than by the sea – a natural contradiction, and almost cheating, if you like. It is quite possible, in mid-August, to set off from Gwaun Vale on Shanks's Pony and walk all day in the Preseli Hills without seeing another human soul. You might spot the odd hill-pony, perhaps, but nothing on two legs. On reflection, this is more a probability than a possibility, and these grand little mountains are tremendous for those striding-out, big-mileage kinds of days.

The valley itself, Cwm Gwaun, is like a lost world, where the 21st century hasn't really had any impact as yet. There is a lane that comes and goes from the valley floor, but it leads nowhere and, not surprisingly, carries very little traffic. Gwaun Vale Touring Park reflects all of this, both in its modest size and in the aura of peace that envelops it.

At first glance there seems to be nothing very remarkable about the site. But once you've pitched and absorbed the view, a quick stroll around the gardens surrounding a children's play area reveals that the site maintenance, or the planting therein, is something of a labour of love by the owner Margaret Harries. Facilities are nicely maintained, with everything on tap to make camping life as stress-free as possible. Despite all this good country air and rural outlook, Gwaun Vale is only just over a mile from the sea, where the briny washes up in the very cute harbour at Fishguard, and plenty of hostelries offer tempting eats and drinks.

From Fishguard, one of the coastal buses, the Strumble Shuttle, can take you off to perfect places for a walk back along the coastal path. While the best way of exploring Cwm Gwaun is on foot, even though it is, admittedly, a little bit hilly in places, it is also a pleasant place for cycling on the traffic-free lanes. Or you can pedal down to Goodwick to catch a ferry to Ireland, for a day out with a difference.

Another unusual place that is well worth the once over is the Castell Henllys Iron-Age Village, near Newport, lying in the shadow of the Preseli Hills. Here they have made a

very believable attempt at reconstructing life in the area as it was lived some several thousand years ago. Perhaps the most impressive and baffling construction in Pembrokeshire, though, is the neolithic burial chamber at Pentre Ifan, standing alone and mysterious on the hills above Cwm Gwaun.

The whole of Pembrokeshire is certainly easily accessible from Gwaun Vale by car, but this place also deserves some serious local inspection, too, so be sure to take your comfiest walking boots.

THE UPSIDE Beautiful, peaceful location with good views and many walking options.
THE DOWNSIDE It's too far away for most of us.
THE DAMAGE £12–18 per night per pitch, depending on season and numbers. Four-legged friends are free.
THE FACILITIES Not brand new or flash, but well maintained and more than adequate, with hot and cold water, flush toilets, free showers, laundry, dishwashing and children's playground.

NEAREST DECENT PUB Bridge End Inn (01348 872545) at Llanychaer, less than a mile down the road, is very much a 'local' sort of pub, where they serve decent pub grub but see very few tourists, so you may end up in the pot with the leeks!
IF IT RAINS You might find better weather on a day trip over to Ireland (www.stenaline.co.uk); nearer attractions include St David's Cathedral and Castell Henllys Iron-Age Village (01239 891319; www.castellhenllys.com).

GETTING THERE From the end of the M4/A40 at Fishguard turn right at the roundabout in Fishguard then immediately right onto the B4313. The site is just over a mile on the right.
OPEN Apr–Oct.
IF IT'S FULL Other good campsites in the area include Ddolwen Farm (01348 873154), across the road from Gwaun Vale, and Morawelon (01239 820565), near Newport, right next to the beach, and handy for several good eating places.

Gwaun Vale Touring Park, Llanychaer, Fishguard, Pembrokeshire SA65 9TA

| t | 01348 874698 | w | www.gwaunvale.co.uk | 7 | on the map |

skrinkle bay

Skrinkle Bay makes a most refreshing campsite find, situated as it is amid the gigantic holiday parks and static caravan cities that litter this part of the Pembrokeshire coastline. In keeping with its humble make-up, just a few subtle green signs point the way to this quiet cliff-top field near Manorbier village, roughly a 10-minute drive from bustling Tenby (Dinbych Y Pysgod).

Skrinkle's utterly basic, back-to-nature feel sets it apart from its gaudy neighbours (none of which are in sight, thankfully) and breathes renewed vigour into any world-weary camper. Well, 'breathes' isn't quite the right word; 'blows' or 'propels' would probably be more apt, as this place is windyyy! Gusts bowl in from the sea, blustering and billowing canvas walls and obliterating any cobwebs that might have crept in to stifle your wilderness instincts.

The exposed upper section of the field is worth a bit of a wind-battering in exchange for the magical coastal and sea views. Pitch up in certain spots, and towards the back of the site, and it looks as though the field drops straight off into the sea. At one side the site dips to form a sheltered alternative area for those not so into the sea view or who don't want to risk the campfire blowing

out. From this corner you can step out of a gate leading straight on to the coastal path, and down further to a set of slanted steps winding their way on to a stony beach.

Sheltered by the raw cliff edges on either side, this beach, known as Church Doors because of the huge door-shaped holes in the rock face, feels neatly hidden away. And when the sea is calm, it's a rather peachy setting for a morning dip, which more than makes up for the lack of showers at the campsite. Bathing in the sea in place of showering – how much more back-to-nature can you get?

If you've indulged your wild side enough and fancy edging back into civilisation, start with Tenby. It's a five-mile walk along the magnificent coastal path from Skrinkle Haven Hostel (the campsite's nearest neighbour). A seaside town in the most classical sense, Tenby has yet to be tarnished by the tourism brush that so often transforms the pretty into the tacky. Granted, behind the old town walls you'll find a fair share of touristy bric-a-brac shops, but these are intermingled with independent clothes, jewellery and antiquey shops that look so inviting, it's impossible to resist stepping into each of these Aladdin's caves. As the town is perched on a large hill, roads wind down from the shops atop the knoll to the beach and town harbour, passing a rainbow of pastel-coloured terraces along the way. Even if it's pouring down with rain you can't help but feel brightened by the cheery colours and atmosphere of Tenby.

It's easy to spend a whole day mooching around the town, fish and chips in hand, stopping off at this little café or that bustling pub. And if the day turns out fine, Tenby's beach, and just about any other on this stretch of coast, offers superb sandy options if you fancy a change from pebbly Skrinkle.

Returning to your cosy tent after a hard day's play is all the more satisfying given Skrinkle's limited facilities. Sitting next to a campfire on a cliff-top perch while the sun sets over the sea before retiring (sans shower) to your temporary night-time shelter fulfils some of those deep-seated desires to live as we once did, without a modern-day creature-comfort in sight. OK, so there's the car, your box of matches and all the nice bits of camping equipment, but let's not be pernickety. Skrinkle has a restorative effect on the soul.

THE UPSIDE 'Wild' camping with fires and sea views.
THE DOWNSIDE No showers.
THE DAMAGE £5 per tent per night and caravans and campers £7.50 per night. Fees are collected daily by the owners.
THE FACILITIES The bare minimum: just 2 portaloos and 2 cold-water taps.
NEAREST DECENT PUB The Castle Inn in Manorbier village is the nearest, but not so decent. Across the road, the Beach Break Tea Rooms are much nicer and have a licence. But for better choice altogether, head to Tenby. The Buccaneer (01834 842273), St Julian St, serves excellent pub grub and has a lovely beer garden. Another good 'un is Bar 10 (01834 845164), St George's St, for a thriving atmosphere and excellent food.

Ocean Restaurant (01834 844536) serves a cracking dinner, too.
IF IT RAINS Head to Manorbier Castle (01834 871394; www.manorbiercastle.co.uk) in the village to inspect a slice of history dating back over 1,000 years. Life-size wax figures in costume are dotted about the place and you can admire the view from the turret windows down to Manorbier's surfer-friendly beach. Adults £3.50, children £1.50 each and dogs are permitted if kept on a lead. Alternatively, head to Tenby, just a 10-minute drive away, to explore its shops and cafés.
GETTING THERE Take the A40 to St Clears then A477 towards Pembroke Dock. At the roundabout take the A478 to Tenby. From Tenby take the A4139 and at Lydstep you'll see a left turn to Manorbier and its castle (on a brown sign). Take this left (on

to the B4585) and carry on until you see a sign for Skrinkle Haven youth hostel and a campsite (in green), turn left here and go straight on, over the mini roundabout by the playground. You'll come to an army barracks at the end of the road; turn left and the campsite is on the right (signposted) just before you get to the hostel.
PUBLIC TRANSPORT There's a railway station at Tenby. From there, take bus 349 to Manorbier village, where it's a mile-long walk to the site.
OPEN June–Sept.
IF IT'S FULL This area of the coast is taken up by vast 'holiday park' campsites and zillions of static caravans, so if Skrinkle Bay is full, the best bet is probably to leave the tent in the car and try the hostel next door. At least you'll still get the view.

Skrinkle Bay, Manorbier, Pembrokeshire SA70 7TT

| t | 01834 871005 | 8 on the map |

fforest

A step, a leap and an icy plunge into the blue lagoon at an old slate quarry make the splashing finale to coasteering, at its Pembrokeshire birthplace. An alternative way of exploring the coastline, coasteering involves using bare hands and trainered toes to scrabble along rocky cliffs, interspersed with jumps into the waves from varying heights. Not for the fainthearted!

Coasteering is one of many endorphin-inducing activities offered by the fforest outdoor team, as part of their 'active relaxation' philosophy; a clever concept that helps clear the mind through learning new skills, and the physical demands of a tough day's play. And it really works. Canoeing down the serene River Teifi, horse-riding, cycling, bushcraft courses and sealife-spotting off Cardigan Island are just some of fforest's sure-fire ways to clear minds of clutter and reacquaint cheeks with fresh air.

fforest outdoor is the brainchild of James and Sîan, who also own fforest at Cilgerran, a slice of the tastiest rural pie, which they thankfully saw fit to share. Sitting in a peaceful pocket of the Ceredigion countryside, this family-run former farm is only a couple of miles' trundle upriver from colourful Cardigan, where the activities team is based. It's the perfect place to unwind and feel soothed by all the good countryside sounds – birdsong, chirping crickets and breeze-kissed boughs – whether you've spent the day cliff-scrambling, shopping, walking or just want put distance between yourself and your normal routine.

Fascinated by what makes a dwelling 'home' rather than simply a place to sleep, James toyed with the idea of installing eco-lodges, before settling on stylish canvas accommodation in the shape of nomad tunnel tents, bell tents, kåtas (tipis) and grand domes all the way from America. And an old barn has been converted into four croglofts – maisonette lodges with beds, sofas and a bathroom.

The dwellings have been dotted around the hilly farmland in fields and among the trees. At night, muted tangerine glows from lanterns lead down to the lodge, which is the communal hub of the place before folk head to the fire pits to watch hypnotic flames over a tasty local beverage from the onsite 'pub'. Adjoining the pub is a makeshift cinema, with straw stacks providing rural pews for guests to enjoy weekly film nights.

This is not just camping; this is fforest camping – a relaxed and comforting tonic to everyday life that easily slips into your being.

Every possible need has been considered: each nomad tunnel tent, tipi and dome has its own 'kitchen' and sits on sturdy wooden decking, from which you can admire picture-postcard views of fields of green and gold sprinkled with languid deer. The decking eradicates any worries about bumpy surfaces, damp and mud that can't help but creep into a tent pitched on the ground. There's wi-fi for those who can't go without

and, for a touch of serious pampering, a sauna (which came flat-packed from Sweden – where else?) is tucked among the trees.

In terms of sanctuary, celeb 'rehab' haunt the Priory has got nothing on fforest. The trowel-loads of care and pride that James and Sîan have put into the place will transform your breathing into long, contented sighs as soon as you arrive.

THE UPSIDE There's nothing not to like here… it's luxurious, relaxed 'camping' in splendid scenery, with lovely staff.
THE DOWNSIDE We had to scrape the barrel to find one and the best we came up with is the distance of some of the domes and nomads to the facilities block.
THE DAMAGE Best to check the website for prices, which range from £175 for a mid-week stay in a nomad tent in April to £800 for a week's stay in a crogloft during the summer holidays. Prices are based on B&B for 2 people. Each additional adult costs £10 per night, £7 per additional child and dogs (maximum of 2 per dwelling) £4 per night.
THE FACILITIES Immaculate. A large wooden block in the tipi and bell tent field with 4 hot showers (and sinks in the cubicles), 4 loos, 4 sinks with Ecover soap and 2 washing-up sinks. Recycling and rubbish bins are nearby, as well as at the lodge. All dwellings have their own kitchen on the decking, with cool boxes, water cooler, crockery, gas hobs and kettle, as well as large bean-bags and comfy chairs. The bell tents, kåtas

and domes are all equipped with indoor stoves and wood, kindling and matches to help keep you snug at night. Traditional Welsh rugs (many designed by Sîan), made from thick wool and hides add to the homeliness of the dwellings. The communal lodge serves breakfast daily and is open in the evenings. On Friday and Monday evenings delicious dinners are served up for those who fancy it, which is a nice way to meet some of your fellow fforest visitors. Sauna and wi-fi, too.
NEAREST DECENT PUB Look no further than the wonderful onsite 'pub' in a rustic old stone farm building next to the cabin. It has a toasty log fire and is lit by candle 'chandeliers', which give the place an ethereal, romantic glow. The slightly smoky atmosphere and hotch potch of seating (ranging from old church pews to benches and wooden stools) help create a really cosy feel. Organic wines and local bottles of beer and cider are sold (added to your dwelling tab).
IF IT RAINS Take your pick from wet activities like coasteering or kayaking with the fforest outdoor team, or head into Cardigan for a mosey

around the shops. Otherwise stay onsite and head for the sauna tucked away in the woods. A rota for its use can be found in the lodge.
GETTING THERE Take the A478 towards Cardigan and at Pen-y-Bryn take a right (signposted 'Cilgerran') next to a church. Just before you enter Cilgerran village take a left onto Church St, then another immediate left signed to the Welsh Wildlife Centre. fforest is on the right just before the centre.
PUBLIC TRANSPORT Train to Carmarthen or Aberystwyth. Buses 460 and X50 leave the respective stations for Finch Square in Cardigan. From here, bus 430 goes to Cilgerran, then it's just under a mile's walk.
OPEN Apr–Oct (but the croglofts are available in the winter months and for Christmas bookings).
IF IT'S FULL Head to Manorafon (01239 623633) on the coast, which is also run by the fforest team. You'll find the same nomad tents and domes there, as well as 4- and 6-berth log cabins in an idyllic seaside setting.

fforest, fforest farm, Cilgerran, Ceredigion SA43 2TB			
t	01239 615209	w	www.coldatnight.co.uk	9 on the map

ty gwyn farm

Did you ever wonder how *Cool Camping* selects the sites that our team of camping sleuths visit, to decide which get 'the nod' and which don't? Well we put our heads together and shake out all the years of accumulated camping knowledge first. Then we check out all the hundreds of recommendations sent in by keen Cool Campers. Finally we assemble a list of 'possibles'. Well, more 'probables', really.

Then one of our number (the youngest one) trawls the Internet day and night searching for new or previously unknown sites and adds them to the list. Usually this covers all the possibles, probables and maybes, but in the case of Ty Gwyn, it was nothing to do with knowledge, or even earnest endeavour by our computer nerd. What happened here was that Cool Camper Number 6 (our oldest and grumpiest) wasn't quite so cool one day in Ceredigion and decided to go for a dip in the sea at Mwnt, near Cardigan. This could very well be the most beautiful beach in Wales, and, after a relaxing swim, No. 6 went for a walk on top of the airy headland, which provides a spectacular view of the coast north around Cardigan Bay.

He was thinking that this may very well be one of the most gorgeous places on the planet and, as he scanned the scene (with his good eye), he noticed a few statics gathered around the nearest farm. His in-built campsite radar then switched itself on and he spotted, perched on the cliffs just a few hundred metres from the most beautiful beach in Wales, a tiny, single green tent. For No. 6, this must have mirrored how the first prospectors felt on the Klondike, in the Yukon, when they struck gold.

Ty Gwyn is that tent and that small group of caravans near the most beautiful beach in Wales. And this place hadn't surfaced either in our collective knowledge or on the Internet. 'There must be a catch' thought our man, so he and the other member of the team (female, first name Attila) dashed off to interrogate the owner, Martyn Evans – poor soul. 'Is this a campsite?' she demanded. 'Well yes' replied Martyn, slightly intimidated and wondering if he had given the right answer. 'Can we stay then?' Attila asked Martyn, and as No. 6 and Attila are not the kind of folk you say 'no' to, he agreed. For quite a while, too, such is the amazing place this site occupies in the landscape.

Ty Gwyn campsite is part of the farm that occupies this remarkable tract of land, plunging so suddenly into the blue dolphin-infested waters of Cardigan Bay. And not forgetting, of course, that it lies next to the

most beautiful beach in Wales. Martyn is just the present and latest generation of the family running the farm and allowing campers to enjoy this remarkable place, where nothing really changes. There has never been any attempt to cash in on the location by advertising, nor any other sort of promotional push. So Ty Gwyn, and its simple pleasures of living in the great outdoors in the most sublime of scenes, remain relatively unknown.

Even if half of humanity did arrive one fine day at beautiful Mwnt (with its tents),

the way the Evans' have set things up ensures that the uncrowded feel of the site will prevail, with just the edges of many, many acres of working meadow mown for camping. Not everyone will love the lack of traditional campsite appearance, but Martyn doesn't necessarily want half of humanity to land up here and will limit numbers, if need be, to preserve the idyllic nature of the place.

In fact we have promised to lend them No. 6 and little Attila to dissuade campers from staying – that is, if too many of you turn up unannounced.

THE UPSIDE The most beautiful beach in Wales is next door, the dolphins can be seen quite close up on most days and the land is managed in an un-site-like way. Then there's the tranquillity, the absolute tranquillity.
THE DOWNSIDE The restricted facilities for campers may put some folk off – no dishwashing – and others may not like the unconventional land management, which places the facilities quite a long way from certain pitches.
THE DAMAGE Tent and occupants £11; electric hook-up £2.
THE FACILITIES Quite basic, but well looked-after, including toilets, showers and hook-ups.
NEAREST DECENT PUB The Flat Rock Bistro at Gwbert Hotel (01239 612638; www.gwberthotel.net) is 4 miles away and offers posh nosh with a fantastic view.

IF IT RAINS Things are better in this respect than may be imagined, but a car will have to be utilised to find wet-weather entertainment. Nearest is the Rainforest Centre, at Felinwynt (01239 810250; wwwbutterflycentre.co.uk), where the grandiose title translates into a very large greenhouse full of butterflies and moths. Cardigan is only a few miles away, while the reconstructed Iron-Age settlement at Castell Henllys (01239 891319; www.castellhenllys.com) is a few miles beyond Cardigan. Cilgerran Castle, near Cardigan (01443 336104; www.nationaltrust.org.uk), Shire Farm Park, near Cardigan (01239 891288; www.leisurefarm.co.uk), fforest outdoor at Cardigan (01239 623633) organises canoeing on the River Teifi, or around Cardigan Island, looking at the abundant wildlife. Trips to Ramsey Island (01437 721423; www.ramseyislandcruises.

co.uk), Solva Woollen Mill (01437 721112; www.solvawoollenmill.co.uk) or the Palace cinema in Haverfordwest (01437 767675) are all options. Or hole yourself up at the Sloop Inn (01348 831449; www.sloop.co.uk) at nearby Porthgain for all-day drinking and eating.
GETTING THERE From Cardigan take the B4548 towards Gwbert, after 1 mile turn right into a lane, then after 2 miles turn right then immediately left onto a narrow lane to Mwnt. Continue past the beach car park to Ty Gwyn.
PUBLIC TRANSPORT Buses service Cardigan and Aberporth, but from there you are on your own or you can get a taxi.
OPEN Early Apr–late Oct.
IF IT'S FULL There is only one other site nearby – Blaenwaun Farm (01239 612165; www.blaenwaunfarm.com).

Ty Gwyn Farm, Ty Gwyn, Min-y-mor, Mwnt, Cardigan, Ceredigion SA43 1QH

| | | t | 01239 614518 | 10 on the map |

tipi west

Tipi West is a true original. Back in 2001, when the idea of tipi tourism was practically unheard of, Brychan Llyr erected the very first tipi at Hendre Farm, on a beautiful hillside spot overlooking Cardigan Bay. As one of the first tipis to grace these shores, it was a primitive affair, offering basic protection from the elements in an authentic structure, but the idea caught on and he expanded to two, three and now four tipis.

Nowadays, it seems that every farmer and his dog is offering tipi accommodation, but whereas some have gone for the 'luxury' end of the market (see p82), with wooden floors, cosy bedding and all mod cons, Tipi West has stuck to its roots, opting for a more traditional approach.

Here, the floors just get a scattering of pine branches and some coconut matting over the slate-covered ground. You get a snug bundle of sheepskins to sit and sleep on, and to help create the vibe of an authentic Sioux camp. And when a fire is lit in the middle of the tipi, you could almost be in the Wild West. The smoke finds its way out of the tent via the age-old ventilation system; air is sucked in through vents at the bottom edge, drawn into the tipi cone and out through the hole in the roof, taking the smoke with it. Or, at least, that's the idea. The reality for the

novice tipi-dweller is more likely to involve a smoke-filled tipi and hours of hearty coughing. On top of this, the combination of open ventilation and thinly insulated stone floors can make these tents feel a little bit nippy, so be sure to bring plenty of extra bedding and perhaps even an airbed or two.

However, with suitable bedding and a certain amount of perseverance in mastering the dynamics of smoke, tipi-camping knocks the socks off the 'normal' version. It feels part bushcraft, part northern plains; Ray Mears meets Big Chief Running Water.

Talking of running water, the requisite facilities can be found in the 'shower shed', tucked away tidily in one corner of the field. But it's the other end of the field that merits a closer look. Beyond the last of the tipis the ground drops away at a healthy angle to reveal a blanket of beautiful green Welsh countryside, a glimpse of the old fishing village of Aberporth and a snippet of the Cardigan Bay sea.

But if this place is beautiful by day, it really dazzles at night, when the fires are lit, the BBQs are sizzling and the citronella candles light the way. Sitting around the fire, with the stars sparkling above and the flame shadows dancing on the white canvas, you might, if the wind's in the right direction, catch the salty scent and the mesmerising swoosh of waves far away in the distance.

Those with romantic leanings should follow the poetry trail around the farm and forest. Brychan's father, Dic (a chaired and crowned Welsh poet), has etched poems into clay tiles and as peiroglyphics on wood pieces as a way of giving something back to the land he farmed all his life.

Brychan also offers horse-riding, in keeping with the western theme, across the open fields and surrounding woodland, but again, this isn't tourist-sanitised. Guests are expected to tack up the horses themselves and get to know their steeds before they set off. At the end of the ride, quite rightly, they help to clean them up again. It's all part of the earthy 'real' Tipi West experience.

For any campers who like a little pampering it should be noted that this is far from a luxury tipi holiday – you can find that kind of thing elsewhere – but it's a thoroughly enjoyable, authentic, back-to-basics place and great value for a weekend.

THE UPSIDE Great-value, rustic tipi accommodation.
THE DOWNSIDE Can get cold, can get smoky.
THE DAMAGE £20 per person, per night.
THE FACILITIES The shower shed houses a shower, toilet and sink, with dishwashing sinks outside. An assortment of crockery and cutlery can also be found in the shed and there's an electricity supply for the kettle and for charging up your phones and cameras.

NEAREST DECENT PUB It's a 20-minute walk along the cliff path to Tresaith, where the Ship Inn (01239 811816; www.shiptresaith.co.uk), although unremarkable inside, offers a panoramic view of picturesque Tresaith Beach from the terrace and good-value, locally caught seafood (mains £9).
IF IT RAINS The interesting county town of Cardigan is about 20 minutes by car. Attractions include the covered market and the Cardigan Heritage Centre (Teifi Wharf, Castle Street; 01239 614404; open daily).

GETTING THERE From Cardiff follow the M4 to Carmarthen, then follow signs to Cardigan. At Newcastle Emlyn follow signs for Aberporth. After the village of Beula turn left at the A487 crossroads near the Gogerddan Arms pub. After 1½ miles, turn right on to Llwyncoed Road, follow the lane past houses and farms, then turn right again for Hendre Farm.
OPEN Easter–end Oct.
IF IT'S FULL Tipis can also be found at Larkhill Tipis (p97).

Tipi West, Hendre Farm, Blaenannerch, Cardigan, Ceredigion SA43 2AN

| | t | 07813 672336 | w | www.tipiwest.co.uk | 11 | on the map |

under the thatch

Camping can be a wildly romantic experience. Picture the scene: two people sheltering from the elements, cooking on a simple fire, enjoying secluded countryside together. And thanks to Under the Thatch, this heady mixture has been elevated to another level entirely.

Under the Thatch specialises in finding derelict or disused Welsh buildings of architectural significance, restoring them to their former glory and setting them up for holiday lets. The idea is to get the buildings contributing to the rural economy, rather than to its decline. The name originates from their first few projects, for which age-old cottages were restored and rethatched in traditional wheat straw, but they've since branched out to other, more unusual, kinds of accommodation, one of them being a beautiful Romany caravan.

The caravan – or 'vardo', to use its correct name – was originally built in 1924 by highly reputable wagon builders Wood Bros and, after years of heavy use and more years sitting in various hay barns doing nothing, was acquired by the gang at Under the Thatch in 2004. They set about restoring it, staying true to the original Romany design and colour scheme. The result is a magnificently authentic holiday time capsule.

The brightly painted wood accentuates the heroic craftsmanship, the bow-top roof curves impossibly – like a bubble ready to burst – and the tiny half-and-half doors need only a large-busted Romany mother leaning out to make them any more authentic.

The cosy interior is similarly themed. A sturdy wooden double bed is built across the back of the caravan, with just enough space for a traditional pot-belly stove and some wooden cupboards in which to stash your stuff. A few steps from the caravan, a rustic cabin is on hand to provide extra storage, as well as a shower, hand basin, toilet and a full range of kitchen accoutrements including fridge and oven. There's even a small sitting area with a CD player, a bit like an extra chill-out room in case the caravan gets too claustrophobic for comfort, or you feel like taking a quick break from your other half.

Both the caravan and the cabin are located in their own small meadow, which follows the banks of the River Ceri, a clean, shallow river perfect for splashing around in of a hot summer afternoon. You might even spot brown trout and otters darting around the waters. From the steps of the caravan, all that can be seen in any direction is green countryside, which adds to the secluded and oh-so-romantic, experience.

It's a short drive to the beaches of Tresaith, Llangrannog and Penbryn, and a slightly longer one to the pretty Georgian harbour town of Aberaeron, with its colour-washed houses and old-time pubs; worth the trip if you feel like a little outing. Three miles east of Aberaeron, the Llanerchaeron country estate, now National Trust, is an 18th-century Welsh gentry holding designed and built by John Nash. The house has already been restored, but just like the mission of the Under the Thatch team, the idea is for the estate to contribute to the local economy by becoming a self-sustaining organic farm.

Since the Romany caravan has become so popular, Under the Thatch have opened up more cosy 'vardos', a shepherd's hut and, have even restored a couple of circus-showman's wagons, any of which are irresistible for all those who fancy a romantic break for two. After all, in a snug wooden room only a few feet wide you won't need an excuse to get cosy with each other.

THE UPSIDE Romany romance, for all soppy types, in a secluded location.
THE DOWNSIDE It's become very pricey.
THE DAMAGE From £210–419 for 4 nights mid-week, £228–299 for a weekend (3 nights), and £323–551 for a week, depending on season. Dogs are welcome to accompany guests.
THE FACILITIES The adjacent wooden shack is set up like a self-catering cabin, so has everything you could need, including a hot shower, fully equipped kitchen and a covered veranda. Fuel is provided for the caravan stove on arrival and an electric blanket is also available if nights get a bit nippy. Bedding is also provided.
NEAREST DECENT PUB The Harbourmaster Hotel (01545 570755; www.harbour-master.com) right on the harbour in Aberaeron is well worth the half-hour drive. It's a foodie's delight, with lobster, crab and fish fresh from Cardigan Bay, local lamb and venison and Welsh Black beef. Bread is baked on the premises. A bar menu is available as well as the restaurant's (mains £12–22). A nearer alternative is the Ship Inn in Tresaith (see p66).
IF IT RAINS Apart from exploring the Ceredigion coast or wandering around Aberaeron, the biggest attraction around here is the National Trust estate at Llanerchaeron (01545 570200; www.nationaltrust.org.uk).
GETTING THERE Directions given on booking.
OPEN All year.
IF IT'S FULL There are two more Under the Thatch Romany caravans: one in the Black Mountains; the other across the water in Ireland. Or for something completely different, camp out in their showman's wagons, shepherd's hut or one of their three retro woodland log cabins at Cenarth. Details available on the website.

Under the Thatch, Romany Caravan, Felin Brithdir, Rhydlewis, Llandysul, Ceredigion SA44 5SN

| e | post@romanycaravan.co.uk | w | www.underthethatch.co.uk | 12 | on the map |

outer bounds

Outer Bounds describes itself as a 'rural retreat' and it's hard to argue with that. The six plots that make up this tiny campsite are dotted among wild split-level land peppered with indigenous willows, oaks, hawthorns and redcurrant bushes. Then there are the wild flowers – the ragged robins, foxgloves, honeysuckle, primroses, stork's bill and dandelions, and the owner's own vegetable patch. Sheep roam the nearby fields and only one or two passing cars might slip along the road each day. Life really doesn't get much more rural than this.

As befits the deepest depths of the countryside, distances to the nearest shop (a surprisingly well-provisioned Costcutter) or pub – both in Llanrhystud – are measured in miles, not metres, four to be precise. If you're walking, set aside a couple of hours for getting provisions and make sure you don't leave anything off your list; it's a long way back to pick up a forgotten pint of milk.

A boutique village of fancy yurts this campsite is not. In fact, as a business venture, it is very much in its infancy. The land has been landscaped sufficiently to allow six sizeable pitches and a shower block has been built, but so far that's your rugged lot. The facilities add a modern design to the site. Based in a charming, brick outhouse, painted aqua blue with tiles in various shades of green, the loos and showers have a Mediterranean funk about them. In August, hot water is available all day, otherwise only in the morning and evening. Low-season campers might have to time their showers, but with so few plots queues will never be a problem. You can always browse the tourist information leaflets if you do find yourself waiting and plan daily itineraries to beaches, market towns, restaurants, art and craft centres and, of course, to the mountains.

Elsewhere, standard-issue campsite basics include a BBQ, a long wooden communal table and cold-water sink for meals and washing up, a washing machine as well as some less conventional features such as a deep well, a view mound for checking out the landscape and, our favourite, a mini stone circle. Bring an acoustic guitar and some incense sticks, set yourself up at the Ridge pitch on top of the hill and on a starry night you'll be in hippy heaven. All of which gives a clue to Outer Bounds' origins...

The owner, Peter, moved here in the late 1960s, joining the invasion of hippies, purchasing ramshackle, rundown homes and farms in the area. Buildings empty since their original owners died fighting in

World War II came to the attention of those dreaming of self-sufficiency and many – like Peter – ended up raising families in the idyllic wild countryside, while allowing friends to camp on their land.

There are people for whom this campsite won't be right. Dog-owners are out of luck; pets aren't allowed because of the risk of worrying nearby sheep. Older children needing the constant stimulation of organised activities could get bored (younger ones will like the nearby Fantasy Farm Park and seaside attractions around Aberystwyth). Glampers who can't camp

without power hook-ups for their TV, DVD, hair curlers/straighteners or cappuccino-frother will find the amenities a little basic. And given the rugged, sloping terrain of the site, wheelchair access is limited.

But anyone looking for the seclusion of countryside calm broken by nothing more than fish-and-chip suppers, trips to the beach (Llanrhystud, four miles away, is a pebbly beach that's great for sunsets) and birdsong – if you think Welsh male choirs are good, wait until you hear their avian counterparts each morning – won't be disappointed by this back-to-basics find.

THE UPSIDE Isolated seclusion with speedy access to coastal walks. Large shoals of dolphins have been spotted gliding by, so get on a boat trip for an up-close-and-personal view.
THE DOWNSIDE As it's a trek to the shops, bring a gas stove and as many provisions as you can carry. Finding the site is tricky after dark; the signs are sometimes blown off their perches. Take a mobile phone to be directed in.
THE DAMAGE £5 per night; £25 per week for adults. £1 per night; £5 per week for children (3–10 years).
THE FACILITIES Six pitches spread far apart offer maximum privacy. Firewood logs £2.75 per bag; kindling 60p for a small bag; £1.75 for a large bag. Two electric hook-ups.
NEAREST DECENT PUB Off the tourist track,

where the locals go, a friendly welcome at the Rhos Yr Hafod Inn (01974 272644; www.rhos-yr-hafod-inn.co.uk), at Cross Inn, is matched by excellent, innovative food and a lovely beer garden.
IF IT RAINS Holidaying with kids? The Fantasy Farm Park ranch (01974 272285; www.fantasyfarmpark.co.uk; entry from £4.75) is minutes away by car and features animals, go-karts and pedalos.
GETTING THERE Find the A487 at Llanrhystud, turn on to the B4337, this is the main 'T' junction, signed for 'Cross Inn'. Travel up the hill approx 1 mile passing 2 left-hand turns, for 'Cwm Wyre' and 'Cwm Mabws'. As the top of the hill becomes visible, you see a turning to the left, with a modern bungalow on your right. Follow this road for approx 2 miles. You will arrive at a crossroads

with a wood yard on your right. Continue over the crossroads for another 50 metres and you will see a turning to the right with a sign for 'Bwlch Gwynt' with a camping symbol – almost there! Follow this for another ¼ mile through a disused farmyard (tarmac road), until you arrive at a small row of cottages on your left. You are here. Someone will be there to show you around.
PUBLIC TRANSPORT Train it to Aberystwyth then catch a taxi for the remaining 20-minute journey (Avril's Taxi: 07743 497700).
OPEN End Mar–end Oct, although advanced bookings may be accepted at other times.
IF IT'S FULL A little further away is the camping hideaway Gwalia Farm (p161), which is equally remote, simple and inexpensive.

Outer Bounds, Bwlch y Gwynt, Llanrhystud, Ceredigion SY23 5EH

| | t | 01974 272444 | e | peter@artizen.me.uk | w | www.campouterbounds.com | 13 | on the map |

the yurt farm

Yurts. Suddenly, they're everywhere. Just a few short years ago they were a rare breed in the Welsh countryside, an exotic novelty. 'Look – there's a yurt! Wow, never seen one of those before.' But then, following the success of pioneers like Trellyn (p31) and Larkhill (p97), Wales has been inundated with these rotund little pods. If you'd lived in Wales pre-yurt, had been away for some years and were now returning home by helicopter, you might well assume (as you surveyed the numerous round tents placed across the countryside like white drafts on a checkers board) that Wales had been invaded in your absence by nomadic tribes from the Central Asian steppe. That's a ridiculous notion, of course, because a) virtually no-one in Wales travels around in a helicopter, except maybe Charlotte Church and b) this invasion is one of UK-ation glampers, not nomadic tribes looking for more fertile terrain. Phew.

But one thing that the UK-ation glamping brigade needs to note is that not all yurts are equal. While many outfits are reputable and well-run (see pages 82–7 for our pick of the yurts and other luxury camping options in Wales), there are also those yurts propped up in fields/back gardens/allotments operated by charlatans who don't really know what they're doing and just want to make a quick buck. You have been warned.

Thankfully, at the Yurt Farm, Thea and Laurie know what they're doing. And they do it very well. This place hasn't been thrown together, it's been thought through, planned out, then nurtured and loved into existence. Breathing new life into a forgotten corner of a large organic farm in Ceredigion, this collection of five yurts is less about the accommodation itself and more about the fully immersing experience of this off-beat, off-grid, off-the-beaten-track hideaway.

A spacious hay meadow gives each yurt as much room as some other campsites might give 30 tents. The yurts are warm and cosy, not to mention impeccably well-maintained. The location is perfect: ridiculously remote and enveloped in the sort of rich, green countryside for which Wales is famous. And the love is evident everywhere: a welcome basket of tasty veg for guests, unique four-poster beds fashioned out of trees and wheelbarrows on hand for transporting your gear (vehicles are not allowed onsite).

The guys here also deserve extra brownie points for making this place as environmentally sensitive as possible. With herb-box fridges, reed-bed drainage, comfy hand-built compost loos and the obsessive use of locally sourced and reclaimed building materials, this canvas commune

is truly low impact with just the sun and the wind for power. Solar panels keep the showers warm while a wind turbine provides enough power to charge torches, but that's it for modern madness.

There's a cosy communal wood cabin with cooking facilities, tables, chairs and board games for rainy days, as well as the wherewithal to make a cup of tea. However, most of your time will no doubt be spent outdoors, with so much space to fill on the farm. In all, there are 150 acres to be discovered, criss-crossed by a network of farm trails and children are free to explore,

make dens, hide in the long grass, play in the sand, hang off rope swings, collect eggs, be licked by cows and gorge themselves silly on the blackcurrants and gooseberries that grow in the yurt meadow.

With the striking Cambrian mountains as a backdrop to this enchanting place, there's no doubt this beautiful, remote location enhances the blissed-out go-slow vibe. But if it's those quirky little yurts that bring you here in the first place, it'll be the welcome, the hospitality and low-impact philosophy that'll keep you coming back.

THE UPSIDE Lovely yurts, lovely people, lovely setting. Lovely.
THE DOWNSIDE Not really a proper downside, but you can't drive on to the meadow. Wheelbarrows available to help you lug your stuff.
THE DAMAGE Weekly rates from £280 (Oct) to £595 (August); short breaks available from £135 in October or £195 at other times.
THE FACILITIES The yurts are exceptionally well equipped with organic futons, bedding, all cooking equipment including gas hob, a basket of farm goodies, a wood-burning stove plus logs and kindling. There are even tea- and coffee-making facilities and a first-aid kit. Outside each yurt there's a BBQ or fire pit and a picnic table. The cabin has a 4-ring gas hob, more cooking

equipment, board games and lots of extra bits and bobs such as toasty sandwich-makers to use on the fire. Next door is the compost loo and solar shower. There's also a sand-pit, swing, a woodshed yurt for extra firewood and an 'honesty' farm shop with meat, veg and jam for sale.
NEAREST DECENT PUB Just over 3 miles away is the traditional Rhos Yr Hafod Inn (01974 272644; www.rhos-yr-hafod-inn.co.uk) at Cross Inn with the tiny windows, thick walls, crackling fires and decorated oak beams that all old pubs should have. Foodies will want to head a bit further to Aberaeron harbour and the delightful Harbourmaster Hotel (see p70).
IF IT RAINS Details of a whole raft of days out can be found in the cabin, including

Oakwood Theme Park (01834 891376; www.oakwoodthemepark.co.uk) and Dolaucothi Gold Mines (01558 825146) where you can try your hand at panning for gold; useful if you're planning an extravagant meal at the Harbourmaster Hotel.
GETTING THERE The site is about 10 miles east of Aberaeron on the A487 and then the B4577 near Penuwch. Full, complicated directions are supplied on booking.
PUBLIC TRANSPORT Pick-ups can be organised if arriving by train or bus at Aberystwyth, Aberaeron, Lampeter or Tregaron.
OPEN Apr–Oct.
IF IT'S FULL For other yurt options see Trellyn Woodland (p31) or our luxury camping feature (p82).

The Yurt Farm, Crynfryn, Penuwch, Tregaron, Ceredigion SY25 6RE

| | | t | 01974 821594 | w | www.theyurtfarm.co.uk | 14 on the map |

How to use our compost toilets

please close the lid after use

SOLIDS
↓ paper
↓ poo
↓ sawdust soak

WEE
Funnel takes wee to the reed bed.

Making sure to take the

sawdust soak. Sprinkle one flower pot full into the tub after a poo.

• sanitary towels
• nappies

bin for anything non-biodegradable

• Please sit down when you use our compost toilet - even if you are a man / boy.
• Please be careful not to block the funnel with toilet paper or sawdust.

luxury camping

If you feel like turning on the style instead of pegging down the nylon, treat yourself to some creature comforts with 'luxury camping'. You deserve it.

It's good to have a treat every now and again: indulge in a bar of chocolate, kick back with a glass of fine wine, go all out on that something you've wanted for aaaages. Well, the same applies to camping. These days, you don't always have to pack your groundsheets, sleeping bags, pegs and – shock horror – tents on your back for an outdoorsy break. There are other options. Comfortable ones.

For thousands of years civilisations across the world have made perfectly comfortable homes out of simple, readily available, materials and easily transportable structures. Many of these have become the inspiration for an alternative camping experience at sites that want to offer a bit more than just a field for people to put their tents up in. In recent years more and more 'luxury' campsites – a handy compromise offering a taste of the great outdoors, but a comfortable one – have opened up their doors to tipis, bell tents, yurts, airstream trailers, shepherd's huts and even gypsy caravans.

Sites offering such different means of accommodation are springing up all over the UK, but in Wales, especially, they have really taken off. We couldn't fit all of them into just one little book, though we've tried with the luxury sites already featured – fforest (p53), the Yurt Farm (p77), Larkhill Tipis (p97), Hidden Valley Yurts (p133) and Strawberry Skys (p167). See over the page for some other suggestions.

Anglesey Tipi and Yurt Holidays

The perfect spot from which to explore the North Walian island of Anglesey; four tipis and one yurt comprise the accommodation at this environmentally low-impact site just a mile from the coast. They sit prettily in a meadow surrounded by trees and wild flowers and come in different sizes to sleep groups, families or couples.

Cae'r Gaseg, Brynteg, Anglesey LL78 8JT; 01248 853162; www.angleseytipis.co.uk; 51 on map

Annwn Valley Yurts

Speckling a wooded valley that's home to an abundance of wildlife are Annwn Valley's Mongolian yurts. Each one sleeps up to five people and has a clear circle in the middle of the roof for star-gazing while you're snuggled up in the cosy interior. Outside is furnished with a BBQ, picnic table and dishwashing area. And for the kids there's a wonderful trampoline to bounce around on.

Pont Cych Mill, Cwm Cych, Newcastle Emlyn, Carmarthenshire SA38 9RR; 01239 698258; www.annwnvalley.co.uk; 52 on map

Ashera Pottery

Just one cosy little yurt set among ash, hawthorn and willow trees on the edge of Gors Fawr Moor awaits you at Ashera Pottery in Pembrokeshire's National Park. A comfortable double and two single futon sofabeds are provided for sitting, sleeping and lounging – when you're not in the onsite pottery studio creating your very own mug while trying not to pretend you're in that scene from *Ghost*.

Mynachlogddu, Clynderwen, Pembrokeshire SA66 7SE; 01994 419278; www.asherapottery.co.uk; 53 on map

The Big Green Tipi

A solitary tipi takes up residence in a small field on the Llyn Peninsula. Living up to its name, it is rather large – sleeping up to 10 people and equipped with one single and two double futons. There are plenty of sheepskins for extra warmth and the central space is taken up by the fireplace, where you can cook or just watch the flames dance. Onsite, children can help tend free-range pigs and collect eggs.

Bryn Awel, Garnfadryn, Gwynedd LL53 8TG 07792 646963; www.biggreentipi.co.uk; 54 on map

Broome Retreat

Two family-sized yurts make up Broome Retreat, in five acres of North Wales' Tanat Valley. Enjoy the surrounding woodland or head off to Snowdonia's National Park to explore its mesmerising beauty and fresh-air-filled activities. If you have a horse or two, they're also welcome here – you can take them on a local horse-course, or just trot along one of the area's many bridleways.

Tyn-y-pant, Penygarnedd, Llanrhaeadr ym mochnant, Powys SY10 0AN; 01691 870398; www.broomeretreat.co.uk; 55 on map

Cledan Valley Tipis

Eight tipis, each with their own name and resembling oversized white witches' hats, are dotted about this Powys valley. Sleeping varying numbers (the Honeymoon, Badger and Woodpecker are perfect for two, while others sleep up to eight) each tipi has a fire pit to keep campers snug.

4 Bank House, Carno, Caersws, Powys SY17 5LR; 01686 420409; www.cledanvalleytipi.co.uk; 56 on map

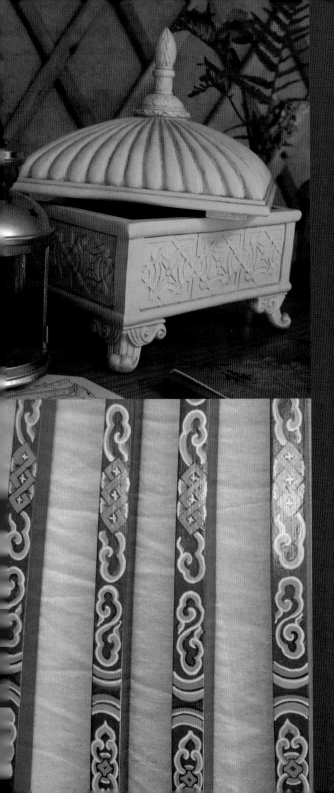

Cosy Under Canvas

Situated near Hay-on-Wye in the wooded Welsh/English borders countryside, Cosy Under Canvas lives up to its name. Each of the four-berth tipis sits on wooden decking to keep the atmosphere within snug and dry. There is a compost loo and solar showers are provided. And guests are welcome to feed their veggie scraps to the onsite pigs and have a look for eggs laid by the chickens and ducks.
Dolbedwyn, Newchurch, Kington, Powys HR5 3QQ; 01497 851603; www.cosyundercanvas.co.uk; 57 on map

Flimstone Farm

Not far from the little town of Narbeth, Flimstone Farm offers accommodation in its farmhouse, family-sized yurt or small campsite. The yurt sits in a corner of the meadow and can sleep up to six. Wall-hangings and bright-orange door and panels provide splashes of colour, while the wood-burning central stove provides heat for warmth and cooking.
Robeston Wathen, Narberth, Pembrokeshire SA67 8EY; 01834 869337; www.flimstonefarmholidays.co.uk; 58 on map

Mandinam Shepherd's Hut

The Victorian farmers who used to sleep in these wooden shepherd's huts when their sheep were lambing surely can't have dreamed that some day they would be classed as 'luxury camping'. But today refurbished huts are being used as a 'different' type of holiday accommodation and this self-contained one at Mandinam, in a glade just outside the Brecon Beacons National Park, is lovely.
Llangadog, Carmarthenshire SA19 9LA 01550 777368; www.mandinam.co.uk; 59 on map

Mill Haven Place

Staying in one of Mill Haven Place's tipis or yurts makes for a luxurious way to enjoy the Pembrokeshire coast. Choose between the yurts Ash and Oak or tipis Sand and Stone and snuggle down for a good night's sleep after a bushcraft session (free with your stay) or day spent on one of the area's golden beaches. The sea views alone make the stay worthwhile. Middle Broadmoor, Talbenny, Haverfordwest, Pembrokeshire SA62 3XD; 01437 781633; www.millhavenplace.co.uk; 60 on map

Pembrokeshire Tipis

Overlooking a valley, these tipis come furnished with rugs, sheepskins and throws to give each canvas dwelling a home-away-from-home ambience. There are onsite cooking facilities as well as a BBQ and outdoor fire, so you can enjoy the best aspects of camping while still being able to climb into a comfy bed after a day's outdoor play. Simpson Campsite, Simpson Cross, Pembrokeshire SA62 6ET; 01437 781972; www.pembrokeshiretipis.co.uk; 61 on map

Tir Bach Farm

Snaking lanes wind their way to this mellow countryside campsite, located on a small farm in Pembrokeshire. If you don't fancy bringing your own tent and pitching on one of their 20 tiered pitches, then you can plump for either of the fully equipped onsite yurts (one sleeping four, the other sleeping six) with their sweeping views and wooden verandas for a proper taste of the good life. Llanycefn, Clunderwen, Pembrokeshire SA66 7XT; 01437 532362; www.tirbachfarm.co.uk; 62 on map

tyllwyd

If you need to get lost, for some reason, then Tyllwyd is hard to beat for remoteness. Squeezed in between the burbling waters of the River Ystwyth and an unclassified road, high in the hills at the top of Cwmystwyth, the site is about 20 miles inland from Aberystwyth. On the map it looks like the back of beyond but, happily, even though Tyllwyd is isolated, it doesn't feel so.

The journey to Tyllwyd takes in a long and winding road, and the nearest supermarket is at Aberystwyth – 20 miles away. So while the site doesn't really feel as though it is in the middle of nowhere, it is probably one of the most isolated campsites in Britain.

Midweek, and out of season, you could set your deckchair up in the middle of the road next to the site and not have to move it all day, but come a summer Sunday it can seem as though every motorcycle and classic car in the world is parading up and down this lonely strip of tarmac. This isn't actually the nuisance it might seem, happening as it does on just a single day, with everybody taking their pride and joy back home by teatime. And nobody is in a rush either – probably because this is one of the most scenic highways in the realm. So, six days a week, those lucky folk camping at Tyllwyd have this lovely road at their exclusive disposal, the joyful sparkling stream of the River Ystwyth to splash about in, an all-round view of the big empty hills of Mid-Wales, and all laid out in a soothing, lush green valley. In a nutshell: location, location, location.

Site facilities are good, too, though you have to cross the road to find them at the farmhouse, which once upon a time was an inn catering for travellers on an important route across Wales. In the 19th century the farmhouse was occupied by the captain of the lead mines, which gave this valley a very different countenance. The present occupiers, the Raw family, are as welcoming as their valley, though it should be noted that their midges offer a less friendly welcome at times. Other, less irritating, wildlife regularly spotted includes red kites, which are now fairly common in these parts. One of the places that the scenic highway leads to, after threading its way through the famous Elan Valley, is Rhayader, where, at Gigrin Farm, hundreds, yes hundreds, of red kites can be seen, grabbing a snack between two and three o'clock every day.

The drive to Rhayader from the site, through the wastes of Wales, may be famously stunning, but the scenery in the other direction, downstream, is more rewarding, being more complex and intimate.

Just a mile or so down the valley the rotting ruins of the abandoned mines have an ethereal and haunting quality about them, and a day spent picking around (carefully of course, with all the usual caveats about children and dogs) in the considerable ruins is exciting for explorers of all ages. The ruins are within easy walking distance and another couple of miles westwards is the Hafod Estate, where way-marked paths wend their way through the woodlands among an ever-changing scene of plunging waterfalls, tall trees, overgrown gardens and flower-strewn meadows.

Plus, there are mountain-biking routes in the forest immediately to the north of Cwmystwyth, and about six miles from Tyllwyd, is Devil's Bridge, where you can climb aboard the train to Aberystwyth. Tyllwyd is in the back of beyond, for sure, but it also feels very much in the centre of Wales.

THE UPSIDE Small country campsite in a scenic, riverside location.
THE DOWNSIDE The midges.
THE DAMAGE Tent and 2 adults £12; extra adult £5; children (5–15 years) £3; electric hook-ups (of which there are 16) £3. Dogs are free, but must be on a lead at all times.
THE FACILITIES Simple but immaculate, with hot and cold water, flushing loos and showers. There are some onsite farm walks now, too. Printed maps are available to borrow from reception, providing a range of walks from a short stroll before supper to a whole day spent wandering or pedalling over the farm's 3,000 acres and mountains.
NEAREST DECENT PUB The Hafod Hotel (01970 890232) at Devil's Bridge, 6 miles away, is a lively and attractive pub. New owners have transformed it into the village hub.
IF IT RAINS Go to Devil's Bridge, examine the waterfalls and take a trip on the narrow-gauge railway to Aberystwyth.
GETTING THERE From Rhayader, follow the signposted road up through the Elan Valley for about 15 miles towards Aberystwyth; Tyllwyd is on the right. Or, from Aberystwyth, follow the A4120 to Devil's Bridge, B4574 to Cwmystwyth, then the unclassified road signposted 'Rhayader'. The site is on the left after 3 miles.
OPEN All year. Booking advisable, particularly in the winter months (to check pitch conditions).
IF IT'S FULL The nearest alternative site is Woodlands Caravan and Camping Park (01970 890233) at Devil's Bridge, 6 miles away – handy for all the goings-on at Devil's Bridge and charmingly eccentric in its own right.

Tyllwyd, Cwmystwyth, Aberystwyth, Ceredigion SY23 4AG

| | t | 01974 282216 | w | www.welshaccommodation.co.uk | 15 on the map |

rhandirmwyn

The Cambrian Mountains is the collective name for a vast but empty area of central Wales. It stretches for 45 miles – all the way from Snowdonia in the north southwards down to Llandovery, where the Brecon Beacons take on the upland mantel in the hilly heart of the country.

In that 45-mile journey, from Machynlleth to Llandovery, you encounter only one main road and the first shop to be seen for miles around – and only a very small one at that – is found at Rhandirmwyn. There are no petrol stations, your mobile phone won't work and the land belongs to the animals. Forty miles without a shop? Not the kind of place for retail addicts, then.

As the damp westerly winds blow in from the Atlantic over this wonderful wild expanse of high, rounded hills, the natural consequence of high rainfall has been exploited by the water companies. Many large reservoirs have been built in the Elan Valley, of which Llyn Brianne is a particularly attractive example. These unnatural lakes have their detractors, but they have, without doubt, allowed much easier access to these lonely places than was previously possible and a chance for the determined to penetrate this last wilderness in southern Britain.

The very civilised Camping and Caravanning Club site at Rhandirmwyn is the perfect basecamp for what amount to almost expeditionary days out in this monumental tract of untouched countryside. The site is a level expanse situated in the bottom of the Tywi Valley, next to the river, with the big green hills rearing up on both sides. It's a lovely place just to sit outside the tent and admire the surroundings, watching the buzzards soar on the thermals. Not that you'll be doing much lounging about, though, not once the alternative options are pointed out to you.

Site facilities are to a very high standard, as is usual with the Camping and Caravanning Club sites, but what isn't quite so typical is just how few folk know about this hidden-away place. Even in the middle of summer, to find this site anywhere near full would certainly be a surprise.

Obviously boots, shoes or sandals (or whatever footwear you walk in) will be useful, with many days of pedestrian exploration on offer, but a bike may prove equally, or possibly more, useful, as the lanes and roads thread startling scenes of all kinds, and the off-road cyclists will find many miles of the rough stuff on the western side of Llyn Brianne.

On the eastern shore of Llyn Brianne the road provides motorists and cyclists with a succession of wonderful vistas right through to Tregaron, with plenty of chances to stop and admire the scene. Wildlife-watchers have things good around here, too, with red kites very easily seen around the lake. If the weather is warm there are some wonderfully inviting swimming pools in the river about six miles upstream, where the water forces its way through a dramatic rocky gorge. Another good swimming spot can be found way, way out in the wilds, but near the road, just above perhaps the most isolated telephone box in Wales, halfway to Tregaron.

This is a very salubrious site in every way, but what it offers, more than anything else, is a gateway to the kind of wild and empty places that seem to be completely alien to the hustle and bustle of modern life, but that most of us feel an instinctive need to communicate with. And the most obvious thing it communicates, in its own natural way, is 'leave your mobile behind'.

THE UPSIDE A great site, in beautiful surroundings, with all sorts of outdoorsy and scenery-watching activities on offer.
THE DOWNSIDE No mobile phone reception. Is that a downside?
THE DAMAGE Adults £5.53–8.17, children £2.45–2.54 or a family deal of £16.34–20.21 (for members only) plus non-members additional £6.46 pitch fee per night. Well-behaved dogs are permitted free of charge, but must be kept on a lead.
THE FACILITIES Excellent, modern facilities with hot and cold water, flush toilets, free showers, laundry, dishwashing and electric hook-ups.
NEAREST DECENT PUB Royal Oak Inn (01550 760332) is just 500 metres away, with decent pub food (curries, goulash, trout from the river) and a selection of real ales including Wadworth and Greene King. If you fancy something really special, it's worth the 13-mile trek to Britain's smallest town, Llanwrtyd Wells, to eat at the Carlton Riverside Restaurant (01591 610248; www.carltonriverside.com). Local produce is championed here, with as many of the mouth-watering meals as possible prepared using locally sourced ingredients.
IF IT RAINS If it rains hard or long enough, the waterspout from the dam on Llyn Brianne is absolutely awesome, otherwise see 'Nearest decent pub' or go and see the unusual sight of a tiny supermarket at Llandovery.
GETTING THERE From Llandovery, follow signs for Llyn Brianne along the unclassified road for 7 miles. At Rhandirmwyn (shop and inn) turn left and look for the campsite after about 500 metres.
PUBLIC TRANSPORT Take a train to Llandovery, and from there either hop into a taxi or walk to Pantycelyn School on Cilycwn Road and catch bus 287 to Rhandirmwyn. The campsite is a 5-minute walk from there.
OPEN Apr–Oct.
IF IT'S FULL Other campsites in the area include a very basic one at Gellifechan Cottage (01550 760397), also in Rhandirmwyn, situated in the even more stunning upper part of the valley.

Rhandirmwyn Camping and Caravanning Club Site, Llandovery, Carmarthenshire SA20 0NT

| | t | 01550 760257 | w | www.campingandcaravanningclub.co.uk | 16 | on the map |

larkhill tipis

In the stillness of the Teifi Valley in rural Carmarthenshire, not far from the bubbling Bargoed stream, can be found the most perfect countryside retreat. And even though it's an entirely artificial invention, from the creative brains and dextrous hands of Tony and Fran Wintle, it feels like the most natural place on earth.

Larkhill used to be just a simple family home surrounded by open farmland. But Fran and Tony had a plan – to turn this place into a peaceful woodland hideaway, far from modern life's stresses and strains. They began planting trees – oak, beech, ash and field maple; in total, 60 different species now cover the land here in what is a remarkable transformation. At intervals, throughout the fledgling woodland, they levelled off terraces and began constructing tipis and yurts in the small clearings, in order to share this quiet corner with guests.

Tony designed and built a hexagonal log cabin, in keeping with the wood-rich environment, to serve as a kitchen and dining room. Through the centre of the land they built an avenue of laburnum trees, which now flowers gloriously every spring in a riot of yellow. At the end of this dazzling walkway, a curious seven-ringed maze is scorched into the earth and, on occasion, it's lit, to become a spectacular labyrinth of fire. A wild-flower meadow occupies the unforested areas of the 20 acres and in addition there are a number of quiet corners and wooded glades hidden around the place – ideal for those who like meditation, contemplation and relaxation.

In essence, Fran and Tony have succeeded in restoring a very small slice of ancient Welsh woodland to its former magical and mystical glory. This is a fantastic example of a low-impact, sustainable tourism initiative, as well as being a great way to make use of redundant farmland.

The care and attention that has been lavished on this place is obvious at every turn. Wooden benches have been hand-crafted and positioned for maximum view-enjoyment. Paving stones have been individually designed, with patterns inspired by nature and the elements. Even the showers, and the electricity at Larkhill, are powered by solar panels and wind turbines, in respect for the environment.

It's an inspiration to see renewable energy being used so effectively; several visitors have even gone on to invest in solar and wind power for their own homes after seeing them in action here.

There are three tipis at Larkhill, each equipped with up to six comfortable single beds, a box full of warm blankets and a central tipi fire hole. The dynamics of the tipi dictate that the smoke should be sucked out through the hole at the top. But the smoke does have a habit of not doing what it should and it can get a bit smoky, so tipis are probably not best suited for families with small kids. The floor is covered in rugs and sheepskins and the foam and futon beds offer a reasonable level of comfort.

The two yurts are similarly furnished, although, not being open to the elements, they are warmer and more weatherproof. A wood stove and a two-ring gas stove are provided in the yurts for heat and cooking.

There are plenty of attractions around here – including a local taste trail, kayaking along the Teifi river and the National Botanic Garden, just outside Carmarthen (Caerfyrddin) – but rushing around isn't really the point of a holiday at Larkhill. It's about chilling out in a wonderfully peaceful valley, sitting around a campfire, enjoying the countryside vistas and listening to the larks of Larkhill calling softly. Sheer bliss. With extra shhh.

THE UPSIDE A peaceful woodland valley; possibly the best tipi setting in Wales.
THE DOWNSIDE Trying to work out how not to fill the tipi with smoke.
THE DAMAGE Tipis and yurts from £60 a night, going up to £520 for a week during the summer holidays. No dogs.
THE FACILITIES Beds, cushions, pillows and extra blankets are included; bring your own sleeping bag, food, towel and torch. Pots, pans, crockery, cutlery and a cool box are all supplied; you can cook on an open fire, the BBQ or on gas hobs. There's also a cooker in the log cabin, along with a sink for washing up and low-voltage power for charging things. Two hot showers are available in another log cabin; you can choose between a surprisingly posh, neutral-smelling compost toilet or a conventional flusher. There's also a small children's play area.
NEAREST DECENT PUB Unfortunately, no outstanding places nearby. For food, the Afon Duad Inn (01267 281357; www.afonduad.com), 3 miles away in Cwmduad, offers a good vegetarian menu and a selection of sturdy Welsh meat dishes. Further afield is the bright-yellow John-y-Gwas tavern (01559 370469), which offers good grub in a cosy bar.
IF IT RAINS Kids can do their own weaving at the free National Woollen Museum (01559 370929; www.museumwales.ac.uk). They also have leaflets at Larkhill about the local taste trail (www.walesthetruetaste.co.uk), the splendid National Botanic Garden (01558 668768; www.gardenofwales.org.uk) and local kayaking.
GETTING THERE Directions supplied on booking.
PUBLIC TRANSPORT Tony will pick up from Carmarthen railway or bus station, 14 miles away.
OPEN The 3 tipis are open from Apr–Oct and the 2 yurts all year.
IF IT'S FULL Another *Cool Camping* site, fforest (p53), provides a selection of tipis, bell tents and domes in an equally magical setting, about a 40-minute drive away.

Larkhill Tipis, Cwmduad, Carmarthenshire SA33 6AT

| | t | 01559 371581 | w | www.larkhilltipis.co.uk | 17 | on the map |

hillend

At the far western edge of the Gower Peninsula, Rhossili Bay, a spectacular four-mile sweep of sand, spreads wide and flat northwards from Rhossili town to the tiny offshore islet of Burry Holmes.

From the elevated vantage point at Worms Head in Rhossili, the sand seems to stretch forever, creating a colossal swathe of surf-kissed beach. You can gain access from Rhossili itself, or at the other end of the beach near the town of Llangennith. There, a narrow country road takes you to the beach car park and to the unassuming surfers' encampment of Hillend.

Occupying some prime beachside real estate behind the grassy dunes, Hillend campsite has had something of a makeover in recent years. After suffering a reputation for lager louts, all-night parties and boisterous teenage gangs from Swansea, the owners decided to make a fresh start.

They designated two of the four fields as 'family only', began turning away groups of dodgy-looking youths and built a 'posh' family café and one of the finest amenities blocks on any Welsh campsite. The result is a site that offers a more amenable, grown-up experience, while successfully retaining its relaxed, surf-cool heritage.

It's a big site, with 275 pitches on 14 acres of level meadowland, but the new shower block can easily cope with the numbers and there's more than enough room for everyone to share the large beach during the day.

Beginners and intermediate surfers will find the conditions at Rhossili Bay perfect, with a combination of the full Atlantic swell and a gently sloping beach producing long waves that can be ridden (well, perhaps, with a bit of practice) for more than 100 metres. The Welsh Surfing Federation (01792 386426; www.wsfsurfschool.co.uk) runs two-hour surfing lessons from £25.

The main draw here undoubtedly has to be the beach, but there are also some spectacular walks that shouldn't be missed. It's possible to walk to Rhossili town along the sands, but better views are to be had if you take the longer, more challenging path over Rhossili Down, starting at the entrance to the campsite. From Rhossili, you can explore Worms Head; a series of headland rocks that take on the appearance of a basking Welsh dragon. It's only accessible for around five hours at low tide, but if you make it safely back, you can enjoy a refreshing drink overlooking the beach from the beer garden at the Worms Head Hotel (01792 390512).

The appeal of this location is more than just the beach, the surf and the Gower landscape; it's much more than the sum of its constituent parts. There's an inexplicable pull about this particular part of the peninsula that has a deep and lasting effect on visitors.

Many of the staff at Hillend originally came here on holiday and just didn't want to leave, taking jobs at the campsite as an excuse to stay. Many more visitors bought holiday homes or ended up retiring here. Maybe it's the wild and remote atmosphere, enhanced by the crashing Atlantic waves. Maybe as the wind stirs up the long-grassed dunes it releases a certain mystical energy. Or maybe it's the fact that the clientele has changed. Whatever the reason, why not start with just a weekend camping at Hillend and see how you go?

THE UPSIDE Surfside campsite with first-class facilities.

THE DOWNSIDE The site is overlooked by a large static caravan park.

THE DAMAGE £15–20 per pitch, per night, including a car and up to 3 people, depending on season and day of the week. There's a £3–5 surcharge for an extra person. The 'no advance booking' policy is a nightmare on summer weekends; your best bet is to get there on Thursday night or send someone down early to reserve and pay for everyone. No dogs.

THE FACILITIES The shower block has 26 showers plus outside showers for surfers, washing-up and laundry facilities. Next door, Eddy's Bistro (usually 8am–8pm, but hours vary) is a coffee shop serving inexpensive meals, dispensing with the need to bring any cooking accoutrements. A shop sells camping essentials, groceries and beach paraphernalia. Eight acres of the site are dedicated to family camping and there is a children's play area, too.

NEAREST DECENT PUB A 5-minute drive or 15-minute walk back up the road is the King's Head in Llangennith (01792 386212; www.kingsheadgower.co.uk), popular with surfers for its music, pool tables and well-priced food.

IF IT RAINS Don't try to use the rain as an excuse for cancelling that surfing lesson. In addition to the nearby options, the Gower Heritage Centre (01792 371206; www.gowerheritagecentre.co.uk) might entertain the kids for a while on a rainy day.

GETTING THERE Hillend is just over a mile west of Llangennith. Pick up the B4295 westwards on the Gower and continue until it hits the sea.

PUBLIC TRANSPORT Bus 116 from Swansea goes to Llangennith, from where it's a hearty mile's walk. Call 08712 002233 for bus timetables.

OPEN Early Apr–late Oct.

IF IT'S FULL Kennexstone campsite (01792 386790; www.gowercamping.co.uk) is a quieter family campsite 2 miles back up the main road.

Hillend, Llangennith, Swansea SA3 1JD		
	t	01792 386204	18 on the map

carreglwyd

As you explore the sleepy village of Port Eynon on the Gower Peninsula, you might be surprised to encounter a bronzed young man whizzing around town on a bright-red quad bike, leg's astride, shirt billowing in the wind and designer sunglasses shielding his eyes. It's a scene straight out of *Baywatch*; though this isn't David Hasselhoff, this is Robert Grove and, rather than making cheesy TV and cheesier pop singles, he's the proprietor of Carreglwyd Camping and Caravan Park.

His confident swagger and *Baywatch* buggy mark him out as a mover and shaker in Port Eynon terms. Indeed, this whole town is dominated by his campsites; his static caravan parks occupy various hillside fields above the town, while Carreglwyd – the tenters' option – has the best position, on the westernmost shores of the bay. On one side of the campsite, a spread of low-tide oyster pools gives way to the sea and sandy Port Eynon beach, while on the other the woods of the headland protect the site from the worst of the weather and the winds.

There are five camping fields at Carreglwyd, with caravans favouring the two nearest to reception for their electrical hook-ups, and tents having the run of the place. The pitches nearest the beach tuck in under the shelter of thick hedges, from where the fields slope very gradually upwards, affording views of Port Eynon bay from the higher ground. All in all, it's a well-organised site, with modern showers that are both clean and free, plus a very good onsite launderette and a small shop at reception with all the usuals. With direct access to the beach as well, it's family-orientated credentials are beyond dispute.

If the sun is a no-show for your camping holiday or if the beach doesn't appeal, head the other way out of the campsite, where a maze of paths explore the headland. They quickly climb to give a panorama of the bay, and you can see down to the campsite and adjacent Victorian lifeboat station, now a youth hostel. This headland is owned and managed by the National Trust, but it feels wild and untamed. There are caves to be found around here as well as Culver Hole, a mysterious four-storey building secreted into the rocks of the headland. Its origin may have been defensive, but it's highly probable that it has seen more use as a smugglers' hideout.

The coastal path from here to Worms Head and Rhossili is a spectacular five-mile walk, showcasing the most dramatic stretch of Gower coastline, taking in sheer cliffs, rocky crags, booming waves and one solitary beachlet. From Rhossili you can continue following the coast to Hillend campsite (p101), a walk that, in its entirety, helps to explain why the Gower was selected as Britain's first official Area of Outstanding Natural Beauty.

The actual village of Port Eynon is a relatively soulless spot. A short row of brash cafés along the seafront have turned deep-frying into a culinary art, the adjacent beach shops are piled high with plastic buckets and inflatable crocodiles, while the coffee shop/snack bar along the main road curiously shuts for lunch. It's a forlorn, forgotten place that only really comes into its own when the sun comes out.

There's no doubt that the main reason for the popularity of Port Eynon is its long, sandy beach, a half-mile crescent with calm, family-friendly waters and water sports opportunities in summer. Lifeguards patrol this beach throughout the summer. If they're ever short on numbers, you can bet Robert would be quick to volunteer.

THE UPSIDE The beach and location.
THE DOWNSIDE The beach and location mean it gets very busy during peak summer.
THE DAMAGE For 2 people, a car and tent, it's £20, plus £8 per extra person. Children 4–10 years are £1 and 10–17-year-olds £2. Dogs are permitted, but must be on a lead at all times.
THE FACILITIES Two modern amenities blocks have toilets, hot showers, basins, laundry and washing-up facilities. Outdoor showers are available for wetsuits. An onsite shop sells groceries and camping accessories. Electric hook-ups and chemical disposal points also available.

NEAREST DECENT PUB Of the 2 distinctly mediocre pubs in Port Eynon, the Smugglers Haunt (01792 391257; www.thesmugglershaunt. co.uk) is marginally more atmospheric. Twelve miles away, in Llanmadoc, you'll find the Britannia Inn (01792 386624; www.britanniainngower.co.uk) with estuary views and locally caught fresh fish on the menu. Main courses range from £10.50–16.
IF IT RAINS It's just under 30 minutes in the car to Swansea, where the Chocolate Factory (01792 561617; www.thechocfactory.com, booking essential) is among the attractions.
GETTING THERE Getting to Carreglwyd is easy. Take the A4118 from Swansea (signposted Mumbles) and follow it all the way to the end. The entrance to Carreglwyd is just by the beach car park at Port Eynon.
PUBLIC TRANSPORT Regular buses run from Swansea directly to Port Eynon, stopping a few metres from the campsite entrance.
OPEN All year.
IF IT'S FULL Back up the hill from Port Eynon is Bank Farm Camping (01792 390228; www.bankfarmleisure.co.uk), a large site with fantastic sea views.

Carreglwyd Camping and Caravan Park, Port Eynon, Swansea SA3 1NN

| t | 01792 390795 | w | www.carreglwyd.com | 19 on the map |

three cliffs bay

Pick up a tourist brochure or guide book to this part of Wales and, chances are, it'll feature a picture of Three Cliffs Bay on the cover. And justifiably so. It's indisputably one of the finest beaches on the Gower Peninsula, with an almost round sandy beach encircled by unique rock formations. A series of limestone peaks rises dramatically into the air, finally disappearing into the Bristol Channel like a retreating monster. It's a distinctive silhouette that has led to claims that this is the 'best view in Wales' and the 'most beautiful bay in Britain', and there's no denying it's a bit special.

As luck would have it, a campsite perches on the high ground behind the beach, quietly taking it all in. Three Cliffs Bay Caravan Park, also known as North Hills Farm Campsite, has been in the Beynon family since 1951, although back then it was sheep and cattle that had the benefit of the views. Five acres of the 150-acre farm are now set aside for camping, providing just enough space for 100 families to camp in peak summer season, although the popularity of the site means that the summer months are not the best time to go.

There are other drawbacks, too – the sloping ground, the fact that not all the pitches

have views and the occasional whipping wind that screeches in from the sea and blows unprepared campers around the site. However, if you're lucky enough to get one of the pitches at the edge nearest the bay, you've certainly acquired one of Europe's finest camping spots. And even if you don't get a view from your tent, the beach itself makes staying here worthwhile.

It's a short scramble down the bank to the beach. Then, if the tide's out, it's a 200-metre barefoot splash across the wet sands to the water's edge. Not only are the cliffs here of unusual formation, but the beach itself is distinctive for the river running through it; a wiggle of tight hairpin bends dissects the sand and meanders seaward in ever-changing patterns. This is the River Pennard Pill that, as you follow it upstream, leads to Pennard Castle, a crumbling Norman fort sculpted into a pleasing combination of derelict towers and soft-edged arches weathered by centuries of wind-blown sand.

Despite its reputation as one of Wales's best beaches, Three Cliffs Bay rarely gets packed, thanks to its relative inaccessibility. From the campsite, it's only a 10-minute walk down to the beach and 20 minutes back up, but non-campers have to take a longer, more circuitous route.

It's worth stressing the point that swimming at high tide can be dangerous due to the currents around the river, but at low tide it's a lovely, relaxing spot for a dip and you may even find inquisitive little fish swimming around you. Dolphins, seals and even basking sharks have been spotted in and around these waters.

The campsite is a highly organised affair. Two onsite wardens keep things in check and the facilities block, a study in 1970s chic with brown-tiled interior and pebbledash exterior, is well maintained. The key to the new family room is closely guarded, but can be borrowed on production of suitably aged children. Pitches are arranged neatly in rows, with caravans to one side of the field, tents to the other, and a separate field is used as a spacious kids' play area for most of the year as well as for additional camping during the busier summer holidays.

No matter how many photos you might see of Three Cliffs Bay, none can match the beauty and majesty of the real thing. Come and experience it for yourself. And, don't forget your camera.

THE UPSIDE The best view in Wales.
THE DOWNSIDE Too busy and crowded in the summer months.
THE DAMAGE Two-person tent £15. Family tent (2 adults, 2 children) £18. Extra adults/children £5/£3. Dogs are welcome at no cost.
THE FACILITIES Well-maintained, centrally located amenities block including disabled and baby-changing facilities. Token-operated showers; 30p for 5 mins. Well-equipped laundry room. Electric hook-ups available. Small onsite shop offers dairy products, frozen foods, drinks and gas exchange. Hard-standing pitches for winter.

NEAREST DECENT PUB There's a super walk from here over the Cefn Bryn hills to the King Arthur Hotel (01792 390775; www.kingarthurhotel.co.uk) 3 miles away in Reynoldston. For a delicious meal, head for the Maes-yr-Haf (01792 371000) in nearby Parkmill. All food is freshly prepared and locally sourced where possible. Draft ales from the Felinfoel Brewery in Llanelli are also worth investigating.
IF IT RAINS The King Arthur pub (see above) is warm and cosy. If you're after something more constructive, then Swansea and the Mumbles are a short drive away. Kids might enjoy the Chocolate Factory (01792 561617; www.thechocfactory.com) in Swansea (booking essential).
GETTING THERE From Swansea, take the A4067 towards South Gower, then the B4436 signposted South Gower and Port Eynon. At Pennard Church, turn right, then next left on to the A4118. Look out for the turning on the left after 2½ miles.
PUBLIC TRANSPORT Regular buses 114 and 118 run past the site from Swansea.
OPEN Apr–late Oct.
IF IT'S FULL Nearby Nicolaston Farm campsite (01792 371209; www.nicholastonfarm.co.uk) also has good views.

Three Cliffs Bay Caravan Park, North Hills Farm, Penmaen, Swansea SA3 2HB

| | t | 01792 371218 | w | www.threecliffsbay.com | 20 | on the map |

grawen

Life's a contrary beast isn't it? And camping at Grawen demonstrates this perfectly. When you find a place so well matched to that camping idyll we all seek – wonderful location, good facilities, a friendly welcome, a relaxing atmosphere – the last thing you want is to spend your time dashing here, there and everywhere doing other things, hardly spending any time at all in this little paradise in the Welsh hills.

Places like this deserve better than being used solely for getting your head down after yet another exhausting day out doing all manner of outdoor things, and attempting to see all the sights with which the Brecon Beacons snares the unwary visitor. No, holidays are for relaxing and time at Grawen should be taken for getting a chair out and admiring the view, strolling around the farm's old stone buildings and – most of all – having an unhurried chat with the other campers, many of whom obviously spend half their lives here.

One of the reasons why Grawen has such a regular clientele, besides all the activities that are going to take you out of a place that begs you to linger, are that the owners, Freda and Gwyn Pugh, must certainly be the friendliest and most helpful of all the campsite owners on Planet Wales. And this isn't just an external show either, for these farming folk are as lovely as the land they tend so carefully.

Grawen is situated at the foot of the southern ridges of the Brecon Beacons' highest hills and some of the most appealing walking country in the land, but even this pales into insignificance once you've run your eyes over the bumpy, hollowy limestone landscape immediately to the west. These valleys, through which flow the Afons (Rivers) Nedd Fechan, Mellte and Hepste, enclose a series of really quite startling gorges, filled with the sound of the rushing rivers and the sight of beautiful shimmering curtains of falling water.

The best way of seeing the falls is to take them all in on one long day. You start from Pontneddfechan and take a circular walk up the Nedd Fechan to Pont Melin Fach, across to the Mellte, then downstream in this steep dramatic gorge, before clambering up and over to the Hepste Valley. Here, another big descent awaits, then back out again before returning to the start. This will be one of those days that will live forever in your personal folklore, such are the scenes you'll have seen and the emotions they'll have provoked. Basic fitness is a must and those with severe vertigo problems may have the odd wobbly moment. It's certainly a hard walk, but nowhere is a bit of suffering more worthwhile than here.

Those with lesser ambition or mobility can still see what is perhaps the most beautiful of the waterfalls by parking at Pont Melin Fach on the Afon Nedd Fechan and walking downstream for half a mile to Scwd Ddwli. Likewise there is a car park handy for the Afon Mellte at Clun-gwyn on the Ystradfellte road. After all this lot you can then get started on the Brecon Beacons, the Brecon Mountain Railway, the Big Pit National Mining Museum and the glory of the Black Mountains, which, all in all, leaves absolutely no time for chewing the cud on this small, friendly and welcoming campsite.

A shame – what's Welsh for *c'est la vie?*

THE UPSIDE A welcome like no other, in beautiful surroundings, with lots to do.
THE DOWNSIDE A lifetime is insufficient to fully explore this area, so what chance is there in a week or two?
THE DAMAGE Tent and 2 persons, £10–12 per night. Extra adults £2. Children under 16, £1. Dogs (on leads at all times, please) £1.
THE FACILITIES Good facilities, including hot and cold water, flush toilets, free showers, laundry, dishwashing; basic foodstuffs sold at the farmhouse and a small children's playground in the camping field.
NEAREST DECENT PUB Nant Ddu Lodge Hotel (01685 379111), 3 miles towards Brecon, has an excellent restaurant. For a quick bite at lunchtime, the Garwnant Visitor Centre, 2 miles towards Brecon, has a nice café and plenty of walking ideas nearby to work off lunch.
IF IT RAINS All aboard the Brecon Mountain Railway (01685 722988) at Merthyr Tydfil, or go high-brow at the impressive Cyfarthfa Castle Museum and Art Gallery (01685 723112), also in Merthyr Tydfil.
GETTING THERE Take the M4 to junction 32 then the A470 to 3 miles beyond Merthyr Tydfil. The campsite is on the left.
PUBLIC TRANSPORT Trains run from Cardiff to Merthyr Tydfil, then the Brecon bus stops near the site.
OPEN Easter–late Oct.
IF IT'S FULL Other *Cool Camping* sites in the area include Priory Mill Farm (p121) and Pencelli Castle (p117).

Grawen Caravan and Camping Park, Cwm-Taff, Merthyr Tydfil, Vale of Glamorgan CF48 2HS

| | t | 01685 723740 | w | www.walescaravanandcamping.com | 21 on the map |

pencelli castle

Once the site of bloody wars and constant fighting, Pencelli Castle is now the site of a grand manor house and camping site belonging to Gerwyn and Liz Rees and their two sons. The manor house was built on the old chapel site of St Leonard's and dates back to 1583, when it was the last remaining building within the castle walls.

The castle was first built in 1080 and was continually altered and rebuilt over the years, until the 19th century, when it was owned by the daughter of Llewellyn the Great, the last Welsh Prince of Wales. After the castle finally fell into disuse, all the stones were taken from the walls and used to build the farms and houses in the local area, so the spirit of Pencelli lives on, albeit in slightly humbler abodes.

You can almost picture the castle as you pitch your tent in one of the three fields: the Orchard, the Oaks or the Meadow. The pick of the three is the Meadow, as it's the largest field and is reserved exclusively for tent campers. All the sites have a backdrop of stupendous views of heather-clad mountains and sheep-strewn, rolling hills, although the drawback is the distance from here to the facilities. The Oaks and Meadow lie in a horseshoe around the old moat, now part of the Monmouth Canal, which

runs alongside the site today. You can even launch your boat or canoe directly into the water from the camping field.

The fields are ancient and spacious, with lots of shady, sheltered spots under some of the biggest and oldest oak trees in the parish. Wooden picnic tables are scattered around – perfect if you feel like having a peaceful meal admiring the view – and there are plenty of water points in all the fields. All in all, this is a well-organised and laid-out site, which is especially good for first-time campers, with flat, sheltered pitches and spotless facilities.

Most people go to the Brecon Beacons for the hiking. All the nearby walking trails are conveniently listed in a booklet written by the owner, who describes himself as 'not a long-distance or serious hill-walker', so rest assured that a gentle stroll means exactly that! Many of the walks are doable from the campsite, although others require a drive to a neighbouring village or town.

A combination of driving and walking will get you to the highest peak in the Beacons, Pen y Fan and, incidentally, the highest point in southern Britain. This walk is probably the hardest in the area, but worth it for the magnificent views from the top. Just remember to take some warm clothing with you and watch the weather.

This is also the area of the Taff Trail, a network of cycle paths that meander along the canals and wind through various villages – and alongside some worthy village pubs, most of which serve great food and even greater local ale. It's a splendid way to spend a sunny day; cycling between pubs, comparing the atmosphere and ales in each. A very refreshing cycle ride.

If that kind of exertion isn't your thing, then there are numerous country markets and fairs to be explored in almost every surrounding town. August sees an internationally renowned jazz festival swinging its way through the parks and theatres of Brecon (Aberhonddu) – www.breconjazz.org – and in October you'll find inspiration for your camping stove at the renowned Brecon Food Festival.

Pencelli Castle is now a place where peace and tranquillity reign. Thankfully it's no longer the site of warfare and carnage so you can sleep peacefully within the castle grounds, Lord of your very own Manor.

THE UPSIDE The views, canal-side situation and justified awards for 'Best Campsite in Wales'.
THE DOWNSIDE Long walk to award-winning loos if camping in the Meadow.
THE DAMAGE £8–10 per person, depending on season; £4.50–6 for 5–15-year-olds. Under-5s are free. Only assistance-dogs are allowed.
THE FACILITIES Spacious, heated showers and baths, heated toilet block, laundry room, fridge-freezers, information room, kiddies' playground, playing field, red deer and pigmy goat enclosure, picnic tables, electric hook-ups, boot and cycle store and wash (bicycles are also available for hire) and shop (stocks gas, bread, newspapers). Chemical disposals/waste-water points. Disabled access, wi-fi, a 'no dog' park.

NEAREST DECENT PUB There are 4 pubs to choose from within a couple of miles. The Royal Oak (01874 665396), literally a few metres away, offers good food and a chance to chat with the locals. For exceptional food, the White Swan (01874 665276; www.the-white-swan.com), 2 miles away in Llanfrynach, is hard to beat, with a changing menu of locally sourced delights in a traditionally styled, but highly polished, pub setting. There's also great food to be had at the Traveller's Rest (01874 676233) in Talybont.
IF IT RAINS You can go boating on the canal with Dragonfly Cruises (07831 685222); try the Brecon Steam Railway Mountain Ride; go indoor climbing at Llangorse Multi Activity Centre (01874 658272) 4 miles away; and try exploring the market town of Brecon, with its own leisure centre (01874 623677).
GETTING THERE From Abergavenny take the A40 towards Brecon, then 6 miles from Brecon turn left to Talybont-on-Usk. In the village, at the T-junction, turn right. Pencelli Castle is 2 miles away, the first place on the right.
PUBLIC TRANSPORT A train to Abergavenny, then bus X43, which runs between Cardiff and Abergavenny, stopping near the Royal Oak pub (see left). Call 08712 002233 for times.
OPEN Open all year except Dec 3rd–28th.
IF IT'S FULL Priory Mill Farm (p121), 5 miles away, is another top spot for exploring the Beacons.

Pencelli Castle Caravan and Camping Park, Pencelli, Brecon, Powys LD3 7LX

| t | 01874 665451 | w | www.pencelli-castle.co.uk | 22 | on the map |

priory mill farm

What do you do when you visit Brecon (Aberhonddu) for the first time and see an old dilapidated farmhouse and mill sitting lonely on the banks of a river? Buy it, that's what. Well, that's what Susie and Noel Gaskell did almost 10 years ago, and they haven't looked back. But then, we're not sure who would in a location like this.

Across the river, woodland belonging to Brecon Priory boasts a rainbow of flowers peeking out through the trees and bushes. And the Grade II-listed (think GCSE A*grade) old stone mill stands grandly at the curve of the river, a relic of Wales's bygone corn- and flour-milling past. Priory Mill is the last mill of the original 12 that used to grace the river banks of this area. The others, including the one at Treiricket (p139) have all been converted into one type of accommodation or another. But Priory Mill, which stopped grinding in the 1930s after the wheel was washed away, is the one exception, thanks to the Gaskells. They fought off developers wishing to buy and convert it so that they were able to slowly restore it to its former working glory.

A furniture craftsman by trade, Noel is passionate about the restoration and is keen to demonstrate that it is still possible to build things as well as they did 300 years ago, when this mill was first constructed. It's a slow process, though, partly because the Gaskells are trying to keep the work as natural as possible. This is partly to protect the rare lesser horseshoe bats that use the river as a motorway, and who like to snooze and have their young in the mill's rafters (doing so even when the mill was running).

But these winged, nocturnal creatures aren't the only guests at Priory Mill, which offers a holiday cottage to rent in the old stables as well as camping in the long, narrow field on the river bank. There are no pitches as such – you are encouraged to set up camp wherever you please, such is the laidback-to-horizontal, nature of the place.

The Gaskells are keen campers themselves and want to maintain a 'small', undeveloped quality here, allowing no more than 30 tents at a time, so that everybody has enough space to spread out, enjoy the sounds of the river and watch the chickens peck about among the fruit trees and tents. Log seats are available to borrow, along with drums for campfires; and the grass is kept in good condition as guests are asked to leave their cars in the teeny car park. At the far end of the field, the path leads down a slope to a small grassy expanse, tucked in a corner by the river, known as the Garden Field

121

because of the border of flowers around its edges. Carry on walking through the field along the path for 10 minutes and you'll find yourself in Brecon, where for a small town there seems to be an awful lot going on, with an independent cinema and theatre and a variety of pubs, cafés, craft shops and galleries to enjoy.

You can stock up on gear from a number of outdoor shops, too, ready to try some of the brisker walks on to the Beacons that are directly accessible from the campsite. Or, if you fancy lazier days, hit the town's fishing shop, then try casting your line into the river at Priory Mill, where it's just £3 for a whole day of fishing.

Priory Mill really couldn't be better located for camping in and exploring the Brecon Beacons National Park. Its very own section of river, access on to the Beacons range for walking, cycling and red-kite spotting and minimal distance into town combine in a boredom-defying choice of things for campers to see and do. If only there were more places like this for sale, *Cool Camping* wouldn't be able to resist buying one, either.

THE UPSIDE Riverside camping, close to Brecon.

THE DOWNSIDE Pitches can get a bit soggy in heavy rain.

THE DAMAGE £7 per person per night; children (11 years and under) £4 each and dogs £1. If you fancy a day's fishing here it's £3.

THE FACILITIES A clean block, hand-built by Noel, with 2 showers and 4 loos (2 each for girls and boys). Metal trays are available to borrow for fires and you can buy firewood and sustainable charcoal (from a local supplier who doesn't use chemicals) onsite, too. There's a 'log seat' collection for campers to borrow for a dry seat.

NEAREST DECENT PUB The Bull's Head (01874 623900) is the first pub you'll hit when you walk from the campsite (just 10 minutes – hurrah!). It's one of the oldest pubs in Britain; small and traditional, serving a good selection of real ales. There's a piano in the corner, where every so often a dab-hand jazz musician will pitch up and tinkle the ivories to the aural delight of drinkers. For food, head to the Felin Fach Griffin (01874 620111) – a 10-minute drive. It's pretty pricey, but the food is sumptuous and they offer an à la carte menu – 3 courses for £27.50.

IF IT RAINS Brecon is a lovely town to explore when the weather's being unfriendly. Follow the Artbeat Trail (www.artbeatbrecon.co.uk) around the cultural hotspots, crafty shops and galleries before stopping at the Café for coffee and a spot of yummy lunch at one of its pretty white tables. Anyone fancying sports over shops and culture can head to Brecon Leisure Centre (01874 623677). The National Showcaves at Dan-yr-Ogof (01639 730284) are well worth a trip, too.

GETTING THERE A40 to Brecon, then travel through the town following the 'through traffic' signs to get on to the 'Struet' road heading north-east out of Brecon towards Hay. Stay on the Struet, keeping the River Honddu on your left. Not long after you've left town and start ascending a hill you'll see a sign for the campsite on the left.

PUBLIC TRANSPORT Coach to Brecon, then a 10-minute walk to the site.

OPEN Mar–Oct.

IF IT'S FULL Head to Grawen (p113) or Trericket Mill (p139).

Priory Mill Farm, Hay Road, Brecon, Powys LD3 7SR

| t | 01874 611609 | w | www.priorymillfarm.co.uk | 23 | on the map |

newcourt farm

The beauty to be found about the Brecon Beacons is no secret and every year many thousands of tourists come to walk the hills, breathe the air and take in the exceptional views. The principal stopping-off point is the town of Brecon (Aberhonddu), from where there's easy access to the most popular routes. Hay-on-Wye (Y Gelli), to the north-east, serves a smaller number of visitors and, again, has well signposted thoroughfares to the hills and a steady stream of walkers. Between these two bustling centres is Newcourt Farm campsite, the launch pad for an altogether different experience of the Brecon Beacons.

A defiantly non-touristy site in a lesser-visited slice of these hills, Newcourt Farm campsite demands some effort on the part of the visitor. Firstly, you'll have to find it; no easy task in a sprawling landscape of narrow lanes. You also have to bring all your own supplies as there's no shop onsite, nor any shop for miles around. And if your aim is to take to the hills, which is pretty much the only item on the agenda here other than sitting in a deckchair and looking out at them, then you'll need an Ordnance Survey map and a compass, as well as some basic orienteering skills. The rewards, though, are worth the effort. Not only does the view from almost every pitch encompass a rich

Black Mountains landscape, but when you do set off to explore, you're likely to have the hills to yourself – a rare treat as far as the Beacons are concerned. The only danger to solitude is the slim chance that you might encounter a gaggle of Duke of Edinburgh-award youngsters, who use this area to test their own orienteering expertise.

The campsite, a hedged field with the thinnest scattering of pear and apple trees, lies within the vast 520 square miles of the Brecon Beacons National Park so, as you might expect, development has been kept to a minimum. However, there is a shower block with disabled facilities, but this is hidden behind a hedge to reduce its visual impact. Even the low-rise corrugated iron farm shed in the middle of the camping field seems less intrusive than it should. Reception is at the cottage over the road. If there's no reply at first, just pitch up and try again later.

After a couple of days out here, though, you may want to reacquaint yourself with civilisation, so taking the six-mile trip to Hay-on-Wye should do the trick. Hay is the self-proclaimed 'town of books', boasting over 30 bookshops and over a million books for sale. Every spring, the town capitalises on its literary reputation by hosting the Hay Literary Festival, a 10-day celebration of literature and arts (p219). Attracting the great and good of the arts world, this oversized festival, for such a small town, boasts a unique atmosphere and is a great time to visit. But festival aside, Hay is also a delightful town in its own right, with galleries, antique shops and more than a few good pubs lining the ancient cobbled streets. It might be a good idea to take a book or two with you to Newcourt Farm campsite, given the lack of decent pubs, restaurants or any other local evening entertainment, but therein lies the attraction of this place. For campers who don't mind a bit of planning, preparation and perseverance, Newcourt Farm is an outstanding countryside site with rewarding walking. For everyone else, contact the tourist offices at Brecon and Hay-on-Wye for the standard campsites and stick to the path well trod.

THE UPSIDE Just a 20-minute walk to the foot of the Black Mountains region of the Brecon Beacons, where fabulous walking is to be had.
THE DOWNSIDE Forgetting something essential.
THE DAMAGE Adults £5, children £2 and under-4s go free.
THE FACILITIES The amenities block has sinks, toilets and hot showers (50p meter). Electric hook-ups are also available, costing £2 per tent and £5 per camper/caravan. The nearest supermarket is in Hay-on-Wye, as is one of Wales's best farm shops, Small Farms (01497 820558), but for all the basics there's a shop in Talgarth.
NEAREST DECENT PUB The Three Horseshoes

Inn (01497 847304) in Felindre is good, but it's worth a drive to Hay, where pub options abound, with Kilverts (01497 821042; www.kilverts.co.uk) topping the lot for atmosphere and menu.
IF IT RAINS Hay-on-Wye is the perfect town for rainy camping days. If you can't find a suitable book to read and a nice café to read it in, then you're not looking hard enough. Water babies (who aren't bothered by a spot of rain) should head to Glasbury for a canoe trip with Wye Valley Canoes (01497 847213) downstream 5 miles to Hay, from where a minibus will transport you back. Anyone still keen for a walk should head for the neighbouring forest, where the trees provide handy protection against the wind and rain.

GETTING THERE Take the A40, then the A470 towards Talgarth and Hay, then at Talgarth turn on to the A4078. When you get to the village of Three Cocks follow signs to Felindre (or Velindre, according to some maps). From Felindre brown 'camping' signs will then point the way to Newcourt Farm.
OPEN Mar–Oct.
IF IT'S FULL The day that this low-key, out-of-the-way site gets full is the day to give up countryside camping. However an alternative venue nearby can be found at Small Farms, aka Lower Porthamel Organic Farm (01874 712125), a working farm where you can pitch the tent in the orchard.

Newcourt Farm, Felindre, Three Cocks, Brecon, Powys LD3 0SS

| | t | 01497 847285 | w | www.newcourt-horseriding.co.uk | 24 | on the map |

llanthony priory

Llanthony Priory resembles a mini Tintern Abbey but, being totally buried in a little-known spot in Wales, amid the enormously gorgeous Black Mountains, it's far less of a tourist trap and, unlike the great ruins of Tintern, has its very own pub attached. Once you've made the tortuous trek through the winding country lanes of the Ewyas Valley and arrived at these antiquated ruins, it's hard to imagine how a small band of Augustinian canons managed to build such a majestic structure way back in the early years of the 12th century. Though, it's easy to see why they chose this spot.

The scenery framing the abbey's ruins is quite simply breathtaking. Great hills clothed in bands of fir trees and decorated in luscious autumnal shades of green, purple and gold tower around, to give the abbey centre stage against a landscape befitting its holy history.

As well as a public bar in the crypts of the abbey and a hotel occupying the priory's former lodgings, Court Farm, next door to the church opposite the priory, has riding stables and a field reserved for camping. Apart from the incredible location of this site, there's nothing especially noteworthy about the place. The facilities stretch only as far as a cold-water tap and access to the public toilets in the nearby car park, so only the most self-contained campers will survive in a hygienic state here.

Facilities-wise, the same can be said for the two other campsites about a mile down the road from the Priory, except that they boast a riverside setting and a good deal more space at busier times: Maes-y-beran Farm, which also sells organic lamb and beef, and another site we're not allowed to mention because the owners want to stay under the radar. This is a shame, as it's our favourite of the Llanthony campsites.

Comprising two spacious fields, it offers camping right next to the river. The ground is flat and the shallow, clean river is paddle-friendly and goes down a treat with kids and dogs alike. Campfires are permitted and a lack of formal 'structure' makes this a laidback gem of a site. There are no facilities here, though – not even a portaloo – so you'll need to take the car up to the public loos at Llanthony Priory when nature calls. It really is back-to-basics camping, but with all the best bits – glorious scenery, a wonderfully relaxed atmosphere and proper campfires.

Back at Llanthony Priory, Court Farm's campsite doesn't allow fires but has the abbey a mere stroll away, as well as the onsite pub, so no wonder it remains popular, despite the lack of facilities and summer-month busyness. This probably has something to do with being able to sit within the ruined abbey with a pint in your hand, or it could simply be the amalgamation of a beautiful setting and all that history oozing from the abbey's stone walls.

Whichever campsite you choose to pitch up at, you're never too far from the abbey and are guaranteed some fantastic walking options, of course, with the imposing, omnipresent walls of the Black Mountains either side of the valley looking interesting, if a little daunting. But once that initial climb is made, the ridge runs off rampantly

for miles without losing or gaining much height. All is not lost if you're no hill-walker, though, as this valley holds a line of secret paths and tracks along its entire length, which lead from one heavenly scene to another. The stroll to Cwmyoy to view the incredible leaning church (honestly, it is unbelievable), and then back again, will be one of life's little highlights. And leaving the confines of this Shangri-La to the west brings you to the second-hand-bookshop town of Hay-on-Wye (Y Gelli) (p126), after which a car-load of books will certainly accompany you back to any of the Llanthony campsites, where the tranquillity can be found aplenty to read them in.

THE UPSIDE Location, location, location.
THE DOWNSIDE Lack of facilities, no advance bookings taken.
THE DAMAGE Varies according to site. Court Farm charges £4 per person and £2 per child per night, Maes-y-beran farm and the other site £3 per person and £1 per child per night.
THE FACILITIES Few and far between. Court Farm has a cold-water tap and there are public toilets (open 24 hours) at the Priory's car park.
NEAREST DECENT PUB The Abbey Hotel (01873 890487) is in the crypt under the Priory ruins, with imaginative bar meals, all served in

unforgettable surroundings.
IF IT RAINS Abergavenny market (01873 735811; www.abergavennymarket.co.uk) usually has something going on with general retail (Tuesday, Friday and Saturday), flea market (Wednesday), collectors' fairs and farmers' market. Hay-on-Wye is 10 miles to the north.
GETTING THERE From the South use the M4 and A449/A470 to Abergavenny, from the North and Midlands take the M5, the M50, and the A40 to Abergavenny, then the A465 towards Hereford, then after 4 miles turn left on to an unclassified road signposted to Llanthony Priory and keep

following the brown signposts. The first campsite you come to is about 5 miles down the road. It has a wooden sign on the gate. Then further up is Maes-y-beran Farm (with a white sign outside), then finally you'll reach the Priory and Court Farm's site.
OPEN All year.
IF IT'S FULL If you'd like facilities, there is a small site at Pen y Dre Farm (01873 890246/07765 050971) on the edge of the Llanfihangel Crucorney village, 3 miles north of Abergavenny, which has a toilet and shower block as well as electric hook-ups.

| **Court Farm**, Llanthony, Abergavenny, Monmouthshire NP7 7NN | t | 01873 890359 | w | www.llanthony.co.uk/camping | 25 on the map |
| **Maes-y-beran Farm**, Llanthony, Abergavenny, Monmouthshire NP7 7NL | t | 01873 890621 | w | www.llanthony-valley.co.uk | |

hidden valley yurts

Hidden Valley Yurts – exactly what it says on the tin. Invisible to, and inaccessible from, the outside world, these homely canvas abodes freckle the green face of a picturesque Monmouthshire valley overlooking a gurgling stream and shielded by trees… But if they're inaccessible, how do you get there? Good question – and one that has a really fun answer.

Guests arrive innocuously enough – by car – which is then abandoned in the car park, often for the entirety of their stay. They then present themselves at the farmhouse, to be warmly greeted by Amanda or Peter, who chauffeur them to their yurt. But this is no ordinary service, as the vehicle in question is an all-terrain buggy, without doors, windscreen – or roof, for that matter.

There are two seats up front and the Ute-style flat-bed trailer at the back is handy for luggage and an extra body or two. As it bounces along the track and down the near-vertical field, one of the two farm dogs bounding happily alongside, it becomes clear why this type of transport is the only wheel way to get to the yurts. It chugs effortlessly along another stony track, across a ford and a puddle or two before arriving at the yurts, which feel miles away from anywhere in their hidden valley.

There are five yurts altogether, stretching higgledy-piggledy along the field, two sleeping five and the other three accommodating up to seven. The yurts' felt roofs and wall linings are 9mm thick and made from pure sheep's wool. Step through one of the brightly coloured doors of these innovative homes to find it lovingly decked with beds, rugs and wall-hangings and equipped with a wood-burning stove and copper kettle, with a bag of kindling for fuel.

The comfortable feel of each yurt entreats you to curl up and unwind, having spent the day wandering around the magical woodland, flower-peppered meadows and fields belonging to the farm's 80 acres. You may even spot one of Amanda's eco-friendly 'pretty lawnmowers' on your travels. No, these aren't machines painted pink, but doe-eyed, woolly alpacas that will happily keep any lawn from getting out of hand.

A designated area of outstanding natural beauty, this corner of Wales, often overlooked in favour of better-known Pembrokeshire and Snowdonia, has been blessed by Mother Nature, and wildlife abounds here. Hidden Valley is home to many species of butterfly, including the uber-rare 'Dingy Skipper' (its name doing this little critter's pretty, patterned wings

a disservice) as well as bees, spiders and bats, so be sure to pack your bug boxes and spotters' guides to do the whole Bill Oddy.

A large wooden, communal kitchen and bathroom area boasts the kind of veranda that would make *Gone-With-The-Wind*-type southerners jealous, and provides just the spot for whiling away evenings lying in the hammock playing a board game. Below the veranda there's a *boules* pitch, campfire area, wood-burning pizza oven and help-yourself herb garden; just some of the thoughtful touches that make this place one of those

extra-special camping experiences that *Cool Camping* can't get enough of.

Within easy reach of Monmouth (Trefynwy), Tintern and other visitable spots along the picturesque River Wye, Hidden Valley is a well-located base for taking in the kind of sites that made the likes of Wordsworth and Turner produce creative masterpieces. But once ensconced in this beauteous valley, snuck away from the outside world, it's hard to tear yourself away. So hard, in fact, you might just wish that the buggy runs out of juice before it takes you back to your car.

THE UPSIDE Luxury camping in the loveliest of locations.
THE DOWNSIDE If you're a couple rather than a family it's a tad pricey to stay at weekends.
THE DAMAGE Each yurt is available for a weekend break of 3 nights or mid-week break of 4 nights. Prices are per yurt and range from £285–320. Also offering couples (or single person) discount for non-peak midweek breaks: £200 for 4 nights.
THE FACILITIES Immaculate and sustainable. There's a large kitchen and communal bathroom 'block' on wooden decking, with picnic tables and hammock, overlooking the valley. The kitchen has all you need and the bathroom has 2 showers and 2 loos. All water comes from a local spring and is flushed away on to a reed bed. There's another kitchen area and rustic compost loos (2) not far off and a small kitchen between the first 2 yurts. The

main kitchen has a breadmaker and built-in BBQ.
NEAREST DECENT PUB Just a mile away (though it's uphill all the way) is the Carpenter's Arms in Llanishen. But you're spoiled for choice in this area, with gastro-pubs the Raglan Arms (01291 690800) in Llandenny, the Hardwick (01873 854220) in Abergavenny, the award-winning Foxhunter (01873 881101) in Nantyderry and Michelin-starred Crown at Whitebrook (01600 860254) – all within half-an-hour's drive.
IF IT RAINS Head for Monmouth, a pretty little town with nice shops and a couple of decent pubs. It's easy to while away a few hours here. Tintern is also fairly near, with its majestic abbey ruins made famous by Turner's watercolour painting and Wordsworth's poem.
GETTING THERE From junction 24 off the M4 take the A449 for 7½ miles, then take the A472 towards Usk and turn right immediately (this is

pretty tricky) on to the B235 signed Chepstow. After a mile you'll reach a fork at Gwernsey; bear left towards Llansoy. Carry on until you reach a crossroads, go straight over (signed Monmouth), then after ¾ mile turn right towards Llangovan on a single-track road. After 2 miles (feels a lot longer) the road turns left. Shortly after this there's a sharp bend to the right, where a track to the left goes off to Lower Glyn Farm – this is your stop, so head down there. The car park is located just above the farmhouse. When you've parked check in at the farmhouse and you and your stuff will be transported in a rugged-terrain buggy to the yurts.
OPEN Early Apr–late Sept.
IF IT'S FULL Dare to head over the border, where you'll find Woodland Tipis (01432 840488) just half an hour away. Featured in *Cool Camping: England* it has the same laidback atmosphere and sumptuous tipis and yurts.

Hidden Valley Yurts, Lower Glyn Farm, Llanishen, Chepstow, Monmouthshire NP16 6QU

| | t | 01600 860723 | w | www.hiddenvalleyyurts.co.uk | 26 | on the map |

Wood For
Campfire
Feel free to collect
dead wood from
the wood's but
Please don't use
this stove wood
on the camp...

trericket mill

The ducks at Trericket Mill have an even better life than their fellow web-toed friends living in the specially built house on that MP's moat. The reason? They live in their very own castle, modelled on none other than the towering turret of the former Norman fortress at nearby Bronllys Castle. The duck-house doesn't quite measure up to the 25-metre-tall Bronllys, but it's a pretty sure bet that these hoi-sin-wary creatures feel rather special returning from a hard day's paddle to lay their heads, and eggs, inside this imposing nest.

Another reason they have it so good here is that there's no danger of being plucked from their castle and ending up *à l'orange* on a Trericket guest's plate. That's because this former mill house has been transformed into a vegetarian B&B, which offers bunkhouse accommodation and camping, to boot. So it's no wonder the ducks and their feathery chicken pals look so at ease as they waddle and scratch about the camping area with chicks in tow.

The campsite comprises just six pitches spread around the orchard across the bridge from the B&B. Despite the fact that it's just off the main road, it is a rather lovely location in which to set up camp – apple trees and picnic tables are spotted about

the place and the fast-flowing waters of the Sgithen Brook run beneath the bridge alongside the site. In the centre, the bunkhouse holds court, with its adjoining loos, showers and outdoor covered kitchen. For anyone wanting to head off camping in winter time, the bunkhouse makes a cosy alternative to nights under canvas if the weather turns a little too frosty. Each with two bunkbeds (so four mattresses), a little corner stove and a couple of pictures, the two bunkhouse rooms are non-fussy, but warm and sheltered enough to guarantee a good, dry night's sleep – essential if you've spent the day canoeing down the river or hiking along the Wye Valley Walk.

Trericket also lies on the Sustrans National Cycle Route 8 (or Lôn Las Cymru), a gargantuan journey spanning the distance between Cardiff (Caerdydd), down south, and Holyhead (Caergybi) up in Anglesey. Pedal southwards from the campsite and you'll take in Brecon and the Beacons, or head north following the River Wye through the hills of Mid-Wales past Builth Wells, where, incidentally, there's a bicycle museum, if you feel like comparing wheels. Either way guarantees some outstandingly green – even by Welsh standards – scenery, thigh-burning ascents and adrenalin-inducing bumpy downhill zooming.

Whether you're heading out for a day in the saddle, on foot or onboard a canoe to paddle your way down river, it's a good idea to start the day with a good, wholesome veggie brekkie at the B&B.

The bean, basil and tomato sausages and nice big pile of wholemeal toast should see you through until lunch, which can also be provided by the B&B, packed up so you can take it with you and enjoy a picnic break. And yep – you guessed it – evening meals are also served there if you're a little too tired to cook up a storm at the outdoor kitchen after a long day out. Takeaway pizzas are another option and taste even better next to a toasty campfire in one of the drums provided.

With all these vegetarian gourmet snacks on hand, any committed carnivores might just be tempted to stray off the meat-eating path on to the veggie track and keep walking. The yummalicious food, coupled with a host of outdoorsy activities on the doorstep of this B&B-cum-bunkhouse-cum-campsite, complete with feathered, castle-inhabiting friends, is enough to transform most guests into happy chickens, or ducks, too. Quackers.

THE UPSIDE Tiny campsite with vegetarian gourmet delights.
THE DOWNSIDE It's directly off the main road, so there is traffic noise.
THE DAMAGE For camping it's £6 per person per night. The bunkhouse costs £12.50 per person and the bunkroom in the mill is £14.50 (both with £5 one-night-only supplement). Dogs are £1 each and must be kept on a lead. Sleeping bags can be hired for £2 a night and towels for £1. Breakfast is £7.50, packed lunches £6.80 and evening meals are from £8. Please pre-book. Wood for campfire drums is £5 for a net of logs; £5 for a bag of charcoal.
THE FACILITIES A couple of hot showers and toilets can be found in the same block as the 'kitchen' and bunkhouse. Across the bridge there's another toilet, but if you're arachnophobic, beware. Vegetarian takeaway pizzas are available from the Mill House, along with tubs of ice cream. The old turbine room makes a super-efficient drying room for any wet clothing.
NEAREST DECENT PUB A 45-minute tramp along the Wye Valley Walk and you'll happen upon the Bridge End Inn in Llyswen (01874 711936). Not outstanding, but a nice enough pub. For another option, head further into Llyswen to the Griffin Inn (01874 754241). Or, for a spot of luxury, head for Llangoed Hall (01874 754525; www.llangoed.com), but only if you have a dinner jacket with you for some seriously posh nosh.
IF IT RAINS A few miles away, Erwood Station Craft Centre is a weird and wonderful place, transformed from a disused old station into a shop selling arts and crafts and a café over 25 years ago. The tracks are still there, sitting beneath an old steam engine, and carriages have been restored to exhibit local paintings, sculptures, jewellery and textiles. It's well worth a wander and, if it stops raining, the station is on the Wye Valley Walk and Sustrans National Cycle Route 8.
GETTING THERE Head towards Builth Wells on the A470. Trericket Mill is situated directly off the main road to the left, between Llyswen and Erwood. There is a signpost, helpfully.
PUBLIC TRANSPORT Take the train to Builth Wells or Llandrindod Wells, then the bus 704 towards Brecon. Running every couple of hours, it will drop off and pick up from Trericket on request.
OPEN Easter–Oct.
IF IT'S FULL Fforest Fields (p151) is much bigger, but has a lake and little streams running through it.

Trericket Mill, Erwood, Builth Wells, Powys LD2 3TQ

| | t | 01982 560312 | w | www.trericket.co.uk | 27 | on the map |

new house farm

There's no point beating about the bush here, because *Cool Camping* readers are a discerning bunch and honesty's always the best policy. So it's probably best to point out right now that the camping at New House Farm is a basic affair.

Situated about a mile down a road heading nowhere (encouraging many an in-car 'are you sure we're going the right way?' conversation until a reassuring sign sporting the word 'campsite' comes into view), New House Farm can be found quietly tucked among the Radnorshire Hills.

Consisting simply of a sloping field to the left of the farmhouse, the campsite is a no-frills setting surrounded by hedges on two sides and a fence separating it from the neighbouring field, home to several rather bored-looking sheep, on the other. It starts to get exciting when you spy the campfire corner at the top of the field; a communal area to save the grass from suffering outbreaks of burnt dark spots, which provides a nice opportunity for campers to get together and bond over a shared marshmallow or two.

It gets even better, though, as hanging near the gate on a noticeboard is an invitation to come and enjoy the home-cooked food served up in the farmhouse's conservatory. And the food in question isn't just any old grub picked up at the local supermarket (actually, this place is so remote, it's unlikely that there's a supermarket within a five-mile radius), but super-fresh ingredients straight from the farm itself.

Sign up for breakfasts, three-course evening meals and even packed lunches, all made from the most local of produce: seasonal vegetables dug up from the garden next to the camping field, meat from pigs, lamb and cattle reared on the farm and fruit picked from the hedgerows and polytunnel. When was the last time you could, hand-on-heart, say you ate a meal entirely sourced from ingredients grown and reared on your doorstep? Well, look no further than New House Farm and shout it loud and proud.

The menu varies according to season and, obviously, every now and again some stray grains of shop-bought rice are going to sneak on to plates. But for the most part it's made up of fresh, organic ingredients that will have your tastebuds somersaulting before you've even picked up a knife and fork. From the simple goodness of spiced parsnip soup and steak and kidney pudding to the more exotic Greek salads and Moroccan lamb dishes, there's always something to tempt the tummy. And when it's time to head home, don't fear: you can stock up on packs of frozen farm sausages, burgers and lamb cuts, as well as any vegetables, salad stuff or fruit that's going.

As much as you may feel like it, you shouldn't really spend your whole time here waiting for the next meal, as there's plenty to do around the area and an activity-filled day is only going to increase that appetite, allowing you to chow down on a few fork-fulls more. The surrounding Radnorshire Hills are well worth getting your boots on for. Blissfully quieter than their rich relations, the Beacons, they retain more of an 'uncharted territory' charm and you won't find nearly so many fellow ramblers to bump

into during your wanderings. A nearby brook provides the perfect racecourse for an army of rubber duckies borrowable from the farm. And it's easy to lose track of time exploring the shops, books and little streets of Hay-on-Wye (Y Gelli) just seven miles away.

Basic the campsite may be, but that's half of its charm; simplicity, peace and campfires in the middle of almost nowhere – aren't they what camping's all about? They certainly provide the key ingredients for a *Cool Camping* dish. Mix in a few spicey extras, like unspoilt countryside surroundings, activities galore and culinary delights on tap, and you've got yourself a new and soon-to-be favourite recipe for country camping.

THE UPSIDE The fantastic home-grown food.
THE DOWNSIDE No public transport and the facilities are pretty basic.
THE DAMAGE Just £3.50 per person per night (campers or caravanners) and under-5s are free. Well-behaved dogs are welcome.
THE FACILITIES Pretty basic and not too clean: An outhouse consisting of 3 loos, one of which has a shower. But hey, this is basic camping, so the facilities aren't going to be spick, span and brand-spanking new. Freezer-pack coolers are available from the farmhouse and, of course, those

scrumptious meals are dished up there, too.
NEAREST DECENT PUB A mile and a half away, in Painscastle, is the Roast Ox Inn (01497 851397; www.roastoxinn.co.uk) serving standard pub fare and a good selection of lagers and ales. But a better option is to BYO drink to enjoy with the farm's excellent evening meals.
IF IT RAINS Head to Hay-on-Wye and stick your nose in some books – there are enough to choose from. Little cafés make sheltering from the weather a pleasant experience, with cosy atmospheres and steaming cuppas. Or brave the rain and hop

into a canoe at Hay's Paddles and Pedals (01797 820604). Another alternative is horse-riding at Bryngwyn Riding Centre (01497 851661).
GETTING THERE Take the A470 to just past Erwood, then take a right on to the B4594 through Painscastle to Rhosgoch, where, at the Herman Chapel, you turn left on to a single-track road and keep going for just over a mile. New House Farm is on the left.
OPEN Easter–late Sept (can be flexible, though).
IF IT'S FULL Trericket Mill (p139) has a similar laidback atmosphere and gourmet (veggie) treats.

New House Farm, Bryngwyn, Rhosgoch, Builth Wells, Powys LD2 3JT

| | t | 01497 851671 | w | www.new-house-farm.co.uk | 28 | on the map |

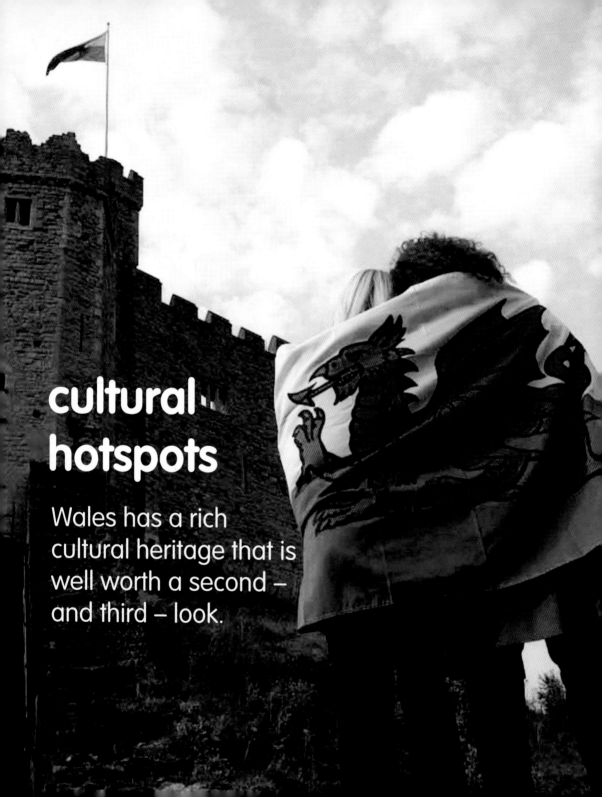

cultural hotspots

Wales has a rich cultural heritage that is well worth a second – and third – look.

Words that usually come after 'Wales' are ones like 'wet', 'mines', 'Tom Jones' and 'leeks'. Hmmm… That paints quite a picture. But, seriously, this country has a rich and diverse history that has led to a unique sense of national identity and a wonderful treasure trove of culture. And what better time to start exploring the story of Wales and Welsh ways of life from past to present than when you're camping in its glorious green valleys, on its golden coastline or high up in its mountains?

There are plenty of quirky regional museums, gallerys and craft centres to visit and enjoy. But the National Museum of Wales (Amgueddfa Cymru) is the big daddy of Welsh cultural hotspots. Passionate about Wales' past and future, the National Museum of Wales differs from other museums through its interactive approach. Visitors aren't simply invited to stare at ancient artefacts, but get to wander around the recreated worlds of the Welsh past and present to see, touch, hear and taste those things that the likes of Roman centurions did centuries ago, right up to the lives led by today's miners.

Turn the page for the lowdown on our favourite cultural experiences.

Big Pit: National Coal Museum

Possibly the most fun museum ever: there's nothing like Big Pit. An underground tour inside a real mine – led by a real, live former miner – this is about as interactive as you can get. Armed with a helmet, headlamp, 'self rescuer' and bulky battery pack, you're lowered 90 metres down the mineshaft for a 50-minute tour you're unlikely to forget and that the kids will love. The miner tour guides are equal parts informative, chatty and hilarious as they lead you along the coal face and tram paths, past the pit-pony stables, and show you the old tools and machinery that were used to work the mine.

Blaenafon, Torfaen NP4 9XP
01495 790311
www.museumwales.ac.uk/en/bigpit/

National Roman Legion Museum

You don't need to go as far as Italy for a glimpse into how the Romans lived – just over the border, in Caerleon, are the ruins of a fortress built back in AD 75 to guard the Empire's furthest-flung outpost: Wales. The National Roman Legion Museum provides a 'get-stuck-in' experience for visitors. Kids can try on replica armour and discover how Caesar's centurions lived. Interactive events include 'Romans in Residence', during which the gardens come alive with a Roman camp. Visitors can join in a proper Roman feast and gamble with the soldiers.

High Street, Caerleon, Newport NP18 1AE
01633 423134
www.museumwales.ac.uk/en/caerleon/

National Slate Museum

Dinorwig Quarry, which closed in 1969, offers an insight into the Welsh slate industry and the lives of the people that fed it. This quarry-turned-museum has a suitably sombre setting. Talks and demonstrations, including live slate-splitting, and restored buildings and machinery help bring the quarry to life. Visitors can roam around the old workshops, real equipment and machinery used to keep this vast quarry churning. There's even a working steam engine that chugs through the site. Wandering inside buildings such as the tiny terraced houses of ironworkers, with interiors restored to three different periods, gives a real sense of the often dark history of this industry and its workers.

Llanberis, Gwynedd LL55 4TY
01286 870630
www.museumwales.ac.uk/en/slate/

St Fagans National History Museum

This 'living' open-air museum is a winner with the kids. Set in the grounds of a 16th-century manor house, St Fagans has over 40 original buildings, including a chapel, school, farm and shops that date back hundreds of years and capture the lives of the people that lived and worked in them. Explore six terraced ironworkers' houses and gardens, each restored to look as it would have in a particular year, the first one set in 1805 and the last in 1985. Live demonstrations from traditional blacksmiths, potters and millers give a fascinating insight into days gone by.

Cardiff CF5 6XB
02920 573500
www.museumwales.ac.uk/en/stfagans/

fforest fields

It's doubtful whether Ralph Waldo Emerson or any of the other great American Transcendentalist thinkers of the 19th century took themselves off camping. After all, equipment wasn't quite so advanced back then. Pop-up tents hadn't even been invented, let alone essential Cath Kidston floral patterns. But if they had ventured out (with giant tent in tow) some of their musings about the human spirit might just have waxed even more lyrical about the euphoric communion between man and nature.

Take the opening chapter of Emerson's essay *Nature*, in which he recommends that if a man (or lady, of course) wants to feel truly alone and at one with the world, he (or she) should 'look at the stars. The rays that come from those heavenly worlds, will separate between him and vulgar things. One might think the atmosphere was made transparent with this design, to give man…the perpetual presence of the sublime'. It sounds a little on the wishy-washy side, but when you're by the long lake at Fforest Fields, looking up at the twinkling night sky, it's easy to see his point, because it is rather magical.

The lake may be man-made, as is the campsite, its pathways, streams and flower beds, but it has been done with such care and taste that even Mother Nature herself would surely give it her blessing. And if you stand in the middle of this campsite and spin around, the natural scenery that greets the eye full circle is just breathtaking – rolling hills in every direction, forests thick with pine trees, grass, ferns, heather and crystal-clear streams…all the finest organic ingredients that make up a melting pot of countryside idyll. The best bit is that you're free to wander off in any one of these directions, because the land (all 550 acres of it) belongs to Fforest Fields.

There is so much walking to be done; over the hills, through the forests and across the moorland. Maps are available at reception to guide you and there's a six-mile way-marked walk to Aberedw village that's well worth doing, not least because it winds up at a terrific pub. Two fishing lakes allow for more sedate activity and the long lake's cool waters make for refreshing swimming or canoeing in one of the site's kayaks. So the chance to commune with nature is at an all-time high here. In fact, not far away, at Gigrin Farm (01597 810243) in Rhayader, there's a red kite feeding centre, where you can get up close to these majestic birds of prey.

The Transcendentalists would be even more thrilled by the opportunities given for the human spirit to shine here, not just in terms

of the tree-hugging and skipping-barefoot-across-the-grass there is to be done, but in terms of trust. Campers are welcome to help themselves to locally produced food, wood and charcoal sold in reception and use the laundry facilities by paying into an honesty box. Such are the natures of the owners and campers that trust and honesty abide at this 100-pitch campsite – hopefully to continue for years to come. Campers can also borrow homemade BBQ/campfire structures to cook on in the evenings, plus games and books to keep the entertainment flowing if it rains.

A haven in the Mid-Wales countryside, it's not surprising that Fforest Fields entices people to return year after year. One gentleman loved it here so much that, after his first visit, he came back every year, always to the same pitch, until he reached the grand old age of 85 – a Cool Camper indeed! Once you've visited, though, it's easy to see the appeal. The natural charms of this place work wonders on the soul and, as Emerson put it, 'In the presence of nature, a wild delight runs through…man, in spite of real sorrows.' He would've just loved it here.

THE UPSIDE The surroundings are stunning and the lake is a magical touch.

THE DOWNSIDE Size. Sometimes you can have too much of a good thing – if there were fewer pitches, this place would be our top choice.

THE DAMAGE Pitches £4.50, adults £3.50, children (under 16) £2.50, babies free; hook-ups £2.50. Dogs are free, but must be on leads and a maximum of 2 per tent/camper van.

THE FACILITIES A block near the reception area with 4 toilets and 3 showers each for ladies and gents. There's a laundry/baby-changing/washing-up room adjacent containing 3 sinks for washing-up and 1 for clothes, 2 washing machines (£3 per wash) and 2 tumble-dryers (£1 per half an hour). The rubbish bin and recycling bins are next to this and have swallows nesting above. There's a telephone box and campers' room behind reception with 2 fridges and 2 freezers (cleaned out every Monday and Thursday), microwave and

6 charger boxes for phones/cameras. These are cunning devices – little lockable tins attached to the walls, with room enough for the charger cables to stick out and be plugged into the wall sockets. They are free, but if you lose the key it's a £20 fine. Shop inside reception for milk, OJ, water, bacon, butter and bread. Games are available for borrowing, as are BBQ/fire drums, and wood and charcoal are for sale in reception.

NEAREST DECENT PUB The Hundred House Inn (01982 570231), ¾ mile away, has a nice atmosphere and does decent food. The Seven Stars Inn (01982 560494) at Aberedw serves fantastic food and lies at the end of the 6-mile way-marked walk from the campsite, so you can build up an appetite and a half on your way there.

IF IT RAINS Head into Builth Wells for a look around the town and, if you fancy seeing a film (or perhaps a play if one's on), there's the Wyeside Arts Centre (01982 552555), which also has

lectures on a variety of topics. For something a bit different there's the National Cycle Collection (01597 825531) at Llandrindod Wells – a bicycle museum with hundreds of different cycles, the oldest of which dates back to 1819.

GETTING THERE If you're heading from the M5, take the A44 then the A481 towards Builth Wells. Fforest Fields is signposted and is on the left, just under a mile from the village of Hundred House. From the M4, take the A40 then the A470 to Builth Wells, pass through the town, then at the roundabout take the third exit on to the A481, Fforest Fields is a few miles down the road on the right and is signposted.

OPEN Easter–end Oct.

IF IT'S FULL There's nowhere else quite like this in the area, but New House Farm (p143) isn't too far away.

Fforest Fields Caravan Park, Hundred House, Builth Wells, Powys LD1 5RT

| t | 01982 570406 | w | www.fforestfields.co.uk | 29 | on the map |

eco retreats

Run by reiki healers ChaNan and husband Michael, Eco Retreats is an upmarket campsite aimed at all those campers who need to take a break from the stresses and strains of modern living. Five fully equipped tipis and a yurt are hidden away in a stunning, remote forest – as a place to chill, you won't find many options that are more horizontal than this.

The site theme is peace and tranquillity, with a healthy dose of eco-living thrown in. To get you in the mood, the camping experience includes an individual session of reiki healing in the comfort of your own tipi or yurt and a soothing meditation as the sun sets. Even the most cynical of campers should give these experiences a try, as they really do transport your mind a zillion miles away from the stresses of life, work, traffic and everything else you might need a relaxing break from.

The drive into the retreat is an amazing experience all by itself, as you negotiate dirt tracks through 600 acres of stunning pine forest and organic farmland. It's hard to believe that such remoteness actually exists in the UK. Towards the end of the drive, you may feel that you're never actually going to arrive, but keep following the hand-painted yellow signs and you'll eventually end up in a leafy glade by a babbling brook surrounded by oak trees. This is probably the last time you'll bother to use your car, until the sad day of your departure, when you'll be desperate to cling to the trees, vow never again to shop for over-packaged goods in supermarkets and declare your allegiance to all things green. The surroundings are so peaceful and calming, you'll just want to stay in the forest for the rest of your life.

The dwellings are furnished in a relaxed, luxurious and romantic way – from sheepskins strewn across the double bed, to tea lights scattered on every surface. A pack of organic edible treats awaits and all the necessary cooking paraphernalia is conveniently to hand. Heating is from both a wood-burning chimenea inside the tipi and an open fire outside. This is particularly necessary when you are running in from the cold spring-water shower – an unmissable, but totally exhilarating, experience.

Each dwelling is set in its own idyllic location, where your only neighbour is the great outdoors. Access is on foot, so it's best not to overdo it on the luggage front. Mountain Tipi is up a steep but short slope, about 10 minutes' walk from your parking spot. Nestled on the side of the mountain, it is sheltered by woodland. The views into the Dyfi Valley are stunning. Here primroses abound in spring and violets take their turn in the autumn.

Meadow Tipi is surrounded by wild flowers in spring, while Waterfall Tipi is a fairly steep 10-minute walk across the river, then up through a wood, carpeted with springtime bluebells. The waterfall is just down the slope and creates a restful soundtrack. Forest Tipi has the most private location. It's a longer, slightly more strenuous walk up a steep hill, but in a breathtaking clearing in the oak forest. The River Yurt, slightly more spacious than the tipis, is nestled down close to the river – an ideal spot for paddling, or even a full dip, if you're up for it.

Also included with an Eco-Retreats break are tickets to the Centre for Alternative Technology (CAT), Europe's leading eco-centre, which is worth a visit on the way home. It offers information and working displays on all things green – from food to washing-up liquid and self-build houses.

Envelop yourself in the total Eco Retreats experience. Leave all your usual gizmos and gadgets at home – don't take your mobile, laptop, radio, iPod or even your guitar. Just doze off listening to the fire crackling – and wake up to birdsong, running water and the wind in the trees.

It's Zen and the art of camping.

THE UPSIDE Luxury dwellings, perfect for couples or family groups, in the most stunning, remote location.
THE DOWNSIDE We'll have to get back to you on that one…
THE DAMAGE A weekend break for 2 is £350, including reiki, meditation, a small organic hamper and a visit to CAT. Last-minute deals are sometimes available.
THE FACILITIES Each tipi/yurt is kitted out with everything you need, except food. A private eco-loo and spring mountain 'shower' are on the doorstep (but if you need a warmer option, solar-shower bags are in every dwelling).
NEAREST DECENT PUB The Wynnstay Hotel at Machynlleth (01654 702941) – a gastro-pub with a great atmosphere (and good food) in the bar.
IF IT RAINS You won't want to leave. But there's always the Centre for Alternative Technology (01654 705950; www.cat.org.uk), the Corris Craft Centre (01654 761584) a couple of miles up the A487; the Museum of Modern Art (01654 703355) at Machynlleth; or tea shops by the beach in nearby Aberdyfi.
GETTING THERE Eco Retreats is hidden in the heart of 600 acres of unspoilt forest. It's a 4-mile journey on 'forestry' roads (which takes about an hour) off the A487. Directions given on booking.
PUBLIC TRANSPORT Trains arrive in Machynlleth about every 2 hours via Birmingham, from where you can be picked up (by prior arrangement) at a cost of £10 each way.
OPEN Apr–Nov.
IF IT'S FULL For a DIY eco-experience (that is take your own tent or tipi) head to Gwalia Farm (p161) in nearby Cemmaes, which offers camping on a lovingly tended organic farm with woodland and a small lake.

Eco Retreats, Plas Einion, Furnace, Machynlleth, Powys SY20 8PG		
t 01654 781375	w www.ecoretreats.co.uk	30 on the map

gwalia farm

When the famous children's author Beatrix Potter visited Machynlleth in 1888 she described the countryside as 'most beautiful, but on rather a large scale for getting about'. Over 120 years later, little has changed. To make the most of pottering (no pun intended) between this wonderful market town, the looming Cader Idris mountain, the various tourist centres and the beaches to the west, you really do need a car.

Potter's young readers and their peers who grew up in these parts harbour idyllic childhood memories of horse-riding, swimming and camping in the wild, but even they needed to be driven around the rural landscape. So if you're intending to pack in plenty of activity during a visit, your trusty feet and bicycles alone won't do, unless you're in training for the Olympics. It's a super-steep mile-long climb to Gwalia from the main A road.

Swimmers will delight at the sandy beaches, just an hour's drive away, and at the indoor leisure centre in Machynlleth itself. Also, in the campsite's grounds there's a pond, complete with its own little pier to jump off. The muddy floor is lined with gravel and parental supervision is required. As for 'wild camping' (pitching your tent in unlicensed spots), this might be popular among locals

in the know, but it's actually illegal on most land. Gwalia to the rescue! Get plotted at one of the country's most primitive campsites in remote countryside, then do nothing and see no-one bar your neighbours until it's time to go home.

This campsite ticks very few of the boxes that many modern-day campers consider vital for a comfortable stay. There are no cooking facilities, amusements, refreshments, nightlights (it's darker than dark here at night) and no showers onsite, though there is one in the house that is shared with B&B guests (you pay £1 and prebook a slot to give time for water to heat up). What you do have here are a couple of flat fields with pitches on the outskirts of an expanse of rushes and a couple of kayaks and a canoe you can use free of charge on the medium-sized pond.

Life here is simple; distractions are non-existent. Since coming here in 1979 the owners have learnt to be self-sufficient. They keep their own chickens in the front yard – camping children can join in feeding and egg-collecting and there are goats that might need hand-milking. Peace reigns more or less until early September, when baby tawny owls are kicked out of their nests and voice their concerns at suddenly being

left to fend for themselves. Surrounded by trees, Gwalia is a blessing for anyone with strong hunterer-gatherer DNA. Campfires are permitted, stray pieces of wood can be picked up and used and the owners sell bundles for £3.30.

Even though there's room for 10 pitches, there's usually just a handful of campers present at any one time and they are spread far enough apart so that all you'll see of your neighbours are wafts of campfire smoke rising from the other side of the rushes. Machynlleth, six miles away, is situated at the head of the beautiful Dyfi Estuary.

Historically, it's the famous location where Wales' rebel leader Owain Glyndwr was crowned in 1404. Today the town is well known for its vibrant Wednesday markets, held at the central Maengwyn Street, where you can pick up arts, crafts and edible organic all-sorts. Do take bikes if you can, though, as three cross-country mountain bike routes start in Machynlleth (Mach 1, 2 and 3), and there's a purpose-built trail, the 'cli-machx', in the nearby Dyfi Forest.

Miss Potter would surely have been proud of you.

THE UPSIDE Cheap camping in the heart of Mid-Wales, close to fantastic hiking trails (Cambrian Way, Dyfi Valley Way and Glyndwr's Way National Trail), and great for mountain-biking and swimming.

THE DOWNSIDE Taking a shower is a mini-mission and, as great as the pond is, swimming with frogs, toads, dragonflies and other insects might not appeal to all.

THE DAMAGE Phone bookings only, £4 adults, £2 children, caravans £140 per week, B&B £25 per person per night.

THE FACILITIES Ten tents can fit comfortably, although the site works best with 6, allowing maximum privacy. There's a flush toilet at the house, two 'earth' toilets in the woods and a spring-water supply. Inside the owners' house a hot shower is available by arrangement, £1 a go, shared with B&B guests. Two kayaks and a canoe are available for free. An old self-contained caravan with a wooden veranda is available for hire.

NEAREST DECENT PUB At the bottom of the hill, sitting on the A470, the Penrhos Arms (01650 511243, www.penrhosarms.com) is a gorgeous stone hotel that serves above-average pub grub at lunchtimes and between 6 and 9pm in the evenings.

IF IT RAINS If the weather's behaving erratically, why not get to the root of it all at the Centre for Alternative Technology (www.cat.org.uk) down the road, which offers solutions to some of the most serious challenges facing the planet.

GETTING THERE Take the A458 from Shrewsbury, follow past Welshpool to the A4970 direction of Machynelith. Turn left after the Penrhos Arms, continue up a steep hill until you reach Gwalia after a mile on the left.

PUBLIC TRANSPORT Train it to Machynlleth then clamber into a taxi, which will cost about £10.

OPEN Twenty-eight days of the year. Send them a request and they'll let you know if they're open.

IF IT'S FULL Outer Bounds (p73), south of Aberystwyth, is similarly wild and ragged, where onsite amusement is of your own making.

Gwalia Farm, Cemmaes, Machynlleth, Powys SY20 9PZ

| t | 01650 511377 | w | www.gwaliafarm.co.uk | 31 | on the map |

strawberry skys

A recent British Household Panel Survey studied a random selection of British citizens to locate the happiest place in the land. The result? Powys, Wales. All that good, clean country living scored highly over cities, whose overcrowded streets and pack-em-in residential blocks were no contest for a county full of sheep and fields. When you meet the proprietor of Strawberry Skys [sic], Eric, the survey rings true; he comes across as someone who jumps into his wellies each morning eager to add the finishing touches to his new glamping paradise.

Eric and Anya decided to drop out of the rat race to buy a smallholding in the British countryside. Cornwall was 'too full'; Scotland too far. Wales was just perfect. Having dreamed up the notion of running a mini yurt empire, they tested out a few established operations before getting to work. Eric admits he owes a lot of his inspiration to Larkhill Tipis (p97), where they stayed for a week. Winds were howling and rains bucketing down, but it didn't put the couple off and in 2008 Strawberry Skys opened for business.

The site is a steep, narrow field facing hills in all directions. Sloping down to a valley floor, the only visible building is a hilltop farmhouse on the horizon. You've just the sheep for company and their job is to graze. Eric's only bone of contention since moving to happy Powys is how fast the grass grows; the sheep help keep the blades short. Situated at the top, middle and bottom of the slope are three Mongolian yurts (two that sleep two people and one sleeping four). Also at the foot of the hill is a fabulous all-mod-cons kitchen outbuilding with a veranda, compost loo hut and hot-shower unit – all of them pretty, clean and new.

Each yurt has been brightly painted in greens and oranges, while solar-powered fairy lights and natural coconut matting join rugs and cushions from India. Wood-burners keep guests toasty during winter months; Eric brings wood around each evening. Fire pits are flanked by chunky wooden tables and benches, and each yurt has its own BBQ. Sitting out all night chewing the fat and chomping on hot dogs under paraffin lamps doesn't get much more stylish than this.

Geographically the location is a winner. Despite being just miles inland from the English border, the site is burrowed deep enough into Wales' bosom to hear the country's provincial, traditional heartbeat.

Yet because it's within reach of motorways, escaping here from most major cities is a breeze. In high season, Eric runs bookings Friday to Monday and Monday to Friday (or both) so no excuse to avoid grabbing a long weekend after a harrowing week in the office. One of the site's big appeals is the concept of taking over the place. Exclusive use for up to 14 adults will set you back £495 for two nights or £900 in high season (a strict-no-noise-after-midnight policy exists here). A few good books, board games and hiking gear are all you need, whether there are two of you, or a dozen.

For a change of scene, yurters can head to one of the pubs in Llanfair Caereinion or Berrieu for lunch or to drop into the butchers to pick up supper. An unmarked footpath runs alongside, though you need good boots, even in the summer, to endure the wet patches of this half-hour walk.

Convenient, cool and waterproof, Strawberry Skys' yurts will be a big hit and bookings are sure to come flooding in. Take it from us; guests could not fail to leave this camp feeling rested, revived and, yes, perfectly happy with life, too.

THE UPSIDE A taste of Wales on the skirts of the England/Wales border; one you can dip into and enjoy all year round.

THE DOWNSIDE This might be a new site, but there are only three yurts, so be quick to bagsy high-season bookings. Cyclists should be aware that the lanes are narrow and therefore dangerous.

THE DAMAGE Two small yurts sleep 2 adults and the larger yurt sleeps 4. Children under 12 are free, additional adults £10 per night. Bookings run for 3 (Fri–Sun) and 4 nights (Mon–Thur) in high season, or both. Prices include firewood/kindling for the fire pits, wood-burners and firelighters. Eggs are sometimes available, free of charge.

THE FACILITIES Two compost loos (one for each movement, as it were), modern kitchen outbuilding, a shower block and, from 2010, a nice terraced picnic area.

NEAREST DECENT PUB Drive out of the top gate, make a right turn, left, then right on to the B4390 towards the 17th-century oak beamed Lion Hotel and Restaurant at Berriew (01686 640452; www.thelionhotelberriew.com) to sample the scrummy fish specials.

IF IT RAINS Take kids to Park Hall Farm (www.parkhallfarm.co.uk), which has lots of indoor play space. No kids? Lucky you: kick back, read a book and enjoy listening to the pitter patter with a strong brew. Or there are shops in Welshpool and Newtown to browse. Or the inside of Powys medieval castle to explore.

GETTING THERE Follow the A458 out towards the coast, signposted Dolgellau/Machynlleth, about 6 miles west of Welshpool, Powys. After 4 miles turn left on to the B4385, signposted Berriew. Take first right, signposted Llanfair

Caereirion/Cwm Golau. Follow this road through a series of bends and you will see the sign for a cross-roads. Turn right on to a single-track lane signposted 'Cyfronyyd'. Drive past the house on the left, round the bend and over the rise. You will only see a farm gate with a small sign marked 'Clyniarth Cottage' when you arrive. Go through the gate and down the steep field until you see the yurts.

PUBLIC TRANSPORT Regular trains run from Birmingham and then it's a short taxi ride (about £10) from Welshpool.

OPEN All year.

IF IT'S FULL Inspiration for this site came from Larkhill Tipis (p97), which has a strong environmental policy.

Strawberry Skys, Clyniarth Cottage, Cyfronydd, Welshpool SY21 9HB

| t | 01938 811308 | w | www.strawberryskys.co.uk | 32 | on the map |

henstent

To be perfectly truthful, there is nothing startlingly different about Henstent – it's a typical small-ish caravan park and it even has a few statics occupying its immaculate acres. However, if you've read the entry concerning the remote and peaceful Pistyll Rhaeadr campsite (p177), but you're still not sure that you can live so simply (or simply can't live with the rules) and if you're still desperate to get intimately involved with he beautiful Berwyn Hills, then Henstent will more than save the day.

Suggesting that Henstent is a bad-behaviour alternative to Pistyll Rhaeadr is being grossly unfair – it's just that Henstent seems to be a bit more 'normal'. You'll get short shrift if you behave badly, but you can quite safely sit outside your tent in the evenings with a glass or two of something. What's more, the Tanat Valley is a very special place, with scenery just as majestic as the Lake District to admire, but with none of the traffic clogging up the roads, nor the crowds covering the hills.

The camping field, if field be the right word (as it's more like a large garden), stands immediately next to the River Tanat, which is usually an affable little river, but in flood would necessitate a wary eye being kept on camping children. The river contains a healthy population of fish and consequently supports a wide variety of wildlife, all of which can be seen from the campsite itself. You might espy otters, though patience will be needed to spot these elusive critters.

The site facilities cover most needs and are well maintained, but be aware that the provision of electric hook-ups doesn't extend to the camping garden.

Another facility that will find favour for many is the proximity to the village of Llangynog, where the number of churches almost equals that of residents. As Llangynog is a former mining village, being close to God was presumably advisable for those involved in such perilous work. There are still visible signs of the mining industry in and around the village and the existence of two ancient pubs, both of which serve decent food, is another indication of busier times in this now sleepy little place.

The Tanat Valley is well suited to several days out on bikes – down one side of the valley, back up the other – as well as a truly great pedalling expedition from the campsite over to the next valley, where Lake Vrnwy can be found and circum-cycled. The valley also offers the chance to have a go at various water sports, with canoe and dinghy hire, plus, if the weather has been typically British in wetness, the chance to go white-water rafting.

Most of all, though, the reason why Henstent is such a great campsite is the scenery in and around the Tanat, which offers walking routes to suit every taste and aspiration. These range from a gentle stroll around the cute neighbouring village of Penybontfawr, to a longer valley walk to the remarkable Penant Melangell church, which as well as

being one of the oldest churches in Britain, is one of the most atmospheric. A slightly harder stroll can, and should, be taken to see the fantastic Pistyll Rhaeadr waterfall (a six-mile return trip), or how about a full-blown traverse of these big, rough, lonely hills – taking in the heights of Cader Bronwen, Cader Berwyn and Moel Sych?

This must be one of the emptiest places in southern Britain and Henstent is a small and civilised oasis from which to explore it.

THE UPSIDE Good facilities; great location.
THE DOWNSIDE A bit on the pricey side, especially for a large family.
THE DAMAGE £8 per adult, children (2–13 years) £3 per night.
THE FACILITIES Hot showers (£1), flush toilets, laundry, dishwashing facilities.
NEAREST DECENT PUB The Tanat Valley Inn (01691 860227) and the New Inn (01691 860229), both in Llangynog, have reasonable food, though nothing very adventurous. Of the two, the New Inn (just 300 years young) will have wider appeal, but

the Tanat Valley Inn retains more of a flavour of the heritage of the area.
IF IT RAINS Try getting even wetter by white-water rafting with Bethania Adventure (01691 870615) at Lake Vrnwy, or visit one of the oldest churches in Britain – Penant Melangell church, near the head of the Tanat Valley.
GETTING THERE From the A5 at Oswestry take the B4580 through Llanrhaeadr-ym-Mochnant, then turn right on to the B4391 through Penybontfawr to the site, on the right just before Llangynog.

PUBLIC TRANSPORT A bus run by the Tanat Valley Bus Company stops outside the campsite gate once a day from Oswestry railway station. Take a look at the times beforehand (www.tanat.co.uk).
OPEN Technically all year, but Oct–Mar it's essential to pre-book as they are prone to winter flooding.
IF IT'S FULL Other great campsites in the area include Pistyll Rhaeadr (p177) or Fronheulog, near Vrnwy (01691 870362), which has a stunning view over the lake, but very basic facilities.

Henstent Caravan and Camping Park, Llangynog, Powys SY10 0EP

| t | 01691 860479 | w | www.henstent.co.uk | 33 | on the map |

pistyll rhaeadr

Waterfalls seem to hold some mystical power over the human gaze and the bigger they get, the more power they have over our fickle spirits. Pistyll Rhaeadr is certainly the highest waterfall in Wales, but its magnetic appeal stems more from the elegant manner of its descent rather than just sheer height.

At Pistyll Rhaeadr, the River Rhaeadr leaps over a ledge in the big, lonely Berwyn Hills and plunges 75 metres towards the sea, pausing briefly in a small pool two-thirds of the way down, then exiting under a beautiful stone archway, to drop again into a deep enchanting pool. This magnificent sight casts a spell on the beholder that must surely have its roots in a basic affinity for water as one of the most powerful and essential elements in giving life to the planet. And yes, this is a campsite guide rather than an emotional or geographical appreciation of Pistyll Rhaeadr. But the essence of the campsite, which gathers around the waterfall's feet, is so tightly bound up with its surroundings and so influenced by this mighty cascade that it must take second place. And to call this a campsite, in the normal sense, would be missing the point.

There has been a campsite here for many generations (since about 1920), along with an Alpine-looking building serving as a

tea room and café, and both fit in with the landscape seamlessly, as if paying homage to the magnificence of nature. Several years ago, however, Phil Pacey, who lived in Norwich at the time, came here for a weekend and fell instantly and totally under its spell. Fate also had it that the café and campsite were up for sale, so he promptly sold up and became the personal property of Pistyll Rhaeadr.

Over the years, the importance of the essence of beauty being a natural miracle changed Phil's approach to running the campsite and he has gradually attempted to educate visitors into leaving behind their urban habits and tuning into a less hectic and more natural way of life, if only for the brief period of their stay. The sign on the site gate now proclaims this place as 'Pistyll Rhaeadr Retreat Campsite' and follows with a few very simple rules of occupancy.

The first one to raise eyebrows is 'no electronic music' – oh, how this is music to the ears – but guitars for campfire singalongs are fine. Another is 'behaviour and respect' – share the peace of this place, don't create a disturbance'. There is also a 'no alcohol' rule (well, the odd glass of wine, or so, is fine, but campers are discouraged from bringing a whole offy's-worth along), on this campsite – so it may not be everyone's cup of absinthe. Then there's the membership scheme to consider, with its annual £25 fee.

Some may think that this fee is a simple device intended to make Phil a richer man but, besides deterring the 'wreakers of campsite havoc', who get habitually thrown off sites after one or two nights, this tends to involve folk more closely in the soul of the place. And it also encourages us all to return to this haven of tranquillity.

Taking the importance of nature a step further, the site also runs, in an adjacent field, weekend seminars with themes tied in closely with the magnificent surroundings. These include meditation, yoga, Satseangs (a journey into your own spirituality) and something called Visionquest, which is too complex to explain here but is desperately simple in practice. These all take place in the huge, colourful yurt, well away from the campsite, so that your peace and quiet won't be compromised. You can even get married in the yurt if you wish. Quietly, of course.

THE UPSIDE Away-from-it-all location in the unspoilt, unknown Berwyn Hills.
THE DOWNSIDE Lack of onsite facilities.
THE DAMAGE £25 annual membership fee, plus £5.50 per person per night; families cost a maximum of £16 a night. Under-3s go free.
THE FACILITIES Very basic, with a single free shower and access to adjacent public toilets, which have hot and cold water to sinks and flush toilets, but the décor is a bit grim. Log baskets are provided for fires.
NEAREST DECENT PUB The Plough Inn (01691 780654; www.ploughcountryinn.com), 4 miles away at Llanrhaeadr-ym-Mochnant, serves a good selection of food and has a games room for whiling away rainy evenings.
IF IT RAINS Oh yes, let it rain – and then that amazing waterfall becomes even more awesome. Otherwise, the National Trust's Chirk Castle (01691 777701; www.nationaltrust.org.uk) is an alternative diversion for an outing.
GETTING THERE From the A5 at Oswestry take the B4580 to Llanrhaeadr-ym-Mochnant, then, in the centre of the village, follow the road signposted for the waterfall.
PUBLIC TRANSPORT Local buses stop at the village, where it's a taxi-ride or walk to the site.
OPEN All year.
IF IT'S FULL The only other site nearby is at Henstent (p173).

Pistyll Rhaeadr, Tan-y-Pistyll, Llanrhaeadr-ym-Mochnant, Powys SY10 0BZ

| | t | 01691 780392 | w | www.pistyllrhaeadr.co.uk | 34 | on the map |

wern isaf farm

Wern Isaf's main reason for being is as a working farm and you'll find it a mere half a mile from the centre of bustling little Llangollen. It's placed at just the right elevation to give the gently sloping camping field an unobstructed view out over the lovely Dee Valley. What may not be apparent from up here is the fact that almost everything you could possibly want to do from a campsite can be done from here. Sceptical? Well, read on.

We'll focus on the surfing first, as it seems the most unlikely for this location, with Wern Isaf being about as far from the sea as it is possible to get in Britain. But surfing it is and it comes in many forms (yes, OK, we're cheating a bit here), with one particular variation being performed in a canoe or an inflatable raft, both of which can be hired, or at least a ride purchased, at the old mill on the River Dee, just down the hill a bit from Wern Isaf.

What next? How about a train ride? Yep, that one is covered by the full-sized Llangollen Railway that chunters up the gorgeous Dee Valley to Carrog. If you really fancy pushing the boat out (on the train?) then book a five-course dinner on an evening trip. Another oddball transport jaunt can be taken by horse-drawn canal boat from the wharf just

down the hill from the site (to a car museum, would you believe?) and a glorious day on the canal can be had by walking or pedalling the three miles from Llangollen to Trevor, where the mighty (and mightily scary) Pontcysyllte Aqueduct carries the canal across the Dee Valley a clear 50 metres above the river. To see is to believe, otherwise the nature and design of this amazing bridge cannot be fully comprehended.

So, that's the water sports, railways and canals dealt with, so how about culture? No cheating needed here, as Llangollen is home to the International Eisteddfod Pavilion, where a varied programme of concerts, films, literary evenings, specialist fairs and festivals are put on just for the benefit of campers at Wern Isaf. That such a small place as Llangollen should house such an important venue seems somewhat remarkable, but it all seems to work out in the end. Bundled up with culture comes religion and, yes, Llangollen has one of the finest religious ruins in the realm at Valle Crucis Abbey.

Moving right along – to stately homes and, again, no problem, with the very pretty half-timbered mansion and lovely gardens at Plas Newydd, on the edge of the town, within easy walking distance of the site.

There are also plenty of pubs and eating houses in Llangollen. You'll find that a week truly flies by in a haze of whizzing here, there and everywhere.

However, despite the embarrassment of entertainment and culinary riches to be feasted upon on foot from Wern Isaf, the most worthwhile walking from here isn't to catch a train, get yourself wet in a canoe, improve your cultural understanding or imbibe necessary life-giving substances. No, because if you walk out of Wern Isaf all those things entail making a left turn,

whereas the most compelling call of all is the scenery, and that means a quick right at the gates. It just isn't any contest.

The whole of the Dee Valley is astoundingly good looking, but just here, behind Wern Isaf, the bare limestone bones of the land poke through in very impressive fashion. The small hill at the back of the site is crowned by the ancient fortress of Castell Dinas Bran – a most picturesque and evocative sight.

So, that's Wern Isaf – cool for everybody for everything.

THE UPSIDE Up in the hills, but still handy for Llangollen.

THE DOWNSIDE It's a steep walk back up the hill from the pub.

THE DAMAGE Adults £6 per night and children £3. Dogs are welcome, but must be kept on leads.

THE FACILITIES Reasonable facilities including hot and cold water, toilets, free showers, laundry, and dishwashing.

NEAREST DECENT PUB The Britannia Inn (01978 860144; www.britinn.com) 2 miles away has an enormous selection of real ales and a good restaurant. Gales Wine Bar (01978 860089; www.galesofllangollen.co.uk) in Bridge Street,

Llangollen, has an unexpectedly good wine list. The Corn Mill (01978 869555; www.cornmill-llangollen.co.uk) is another good 'un, perched on a spectacular riverside spot.

IF IT RAINS Choose from Plas Newydd (01978 861314; infoline: 01248 715272; www.nationaltrust.org.uk) and JJ Canoeing and Rafting (01978 860763; www.jjraftcanoe.com). Or try the Llangollen Railway, including Dinner in the Diner on the Berwyn Belle (01978 860979); and the Llangollen Wharf horse-drawn canal cruises (01978 860702; www.horsedrawnboats.co.uk).

GETTING THERE Take the A5 or the A483/A5 to Llangollen then, in the centre of town, turn right

at the lights, cross the river, right at the junction then immediately left into a lane, right at the next junction (still with us?), then it's up the hill on the right.

PUBLIC TRANSPORT Take a train to Chester or Wrexham, then the local bus service to Llangollen.

OPEN Easter/Apr–Oct.

IF IT'S FULL Another countrified campsite within striking distance is Tower Farm (07971 340559; www.towerfarmholidays.co.uk).

Wern Isaf Farm, Llangollen, Denbighshire LL20 8DU

| | t | 01978 860632 | w | www.wernisaf.co.uk | 35 | on the map |

cae du

'Away from it all', 'a wonderful sea view', 'an idyllic location' and 'well-maintained' are all terms that can be fairly applied in a bid to describe Cae Du. But it's not enough, and to see this place for the first time, approaching from the north on the A493, your little heart skips a beat or two. For there, a couple of hundred metres below, lying right next to the sea, with an unspoilt landscape enveloping it, is the campsite of your dreams.

It looks like a place that has become detached from the real world and it proves to be just that. If all you want from your camping break is a watery landscape and an escape from the mad world we all live in, then this is the perfect place to unwind to the rhythms of the waves and the tides. 'Idyllic' is a word that is used far too often, but it sums up the situation of Cae Du as no other word can.

As for the details – the actual logistics of camping at Cae Du – suffice to say that the facilities are excellent, although level pitches are a bit thin on the ground (so active sleepers may end up rolling into the sea), and the washing-up sink is perfectly placed for taking in the most incredible view as you bubble and scrub away. But while Cae Du is an escape from the rat race, it isn't so far removed that there is nothing else to do, if

staring out to sea doesn't hold your attention for the entire holiday. Or if the children start walking around with placards round their necks protesting their need for action. Or if the weather turns a bit wild on this exposed stretch of coastline – which it can do. What you can't fail to notice is that every hour and a half a train rides through the site, on its way to either Shrewsbury or Pwllheli, depending on which direction it's going. And you get to thinking that if this coastline is so devilishly handsome then this railway journey may be a very good idea. And it is.

It's about a mile to the nearest station on foot and from there a whole new world awaits you: Shrewsbury, which must be one of the most handsome old towns in Britain; a short hop of three miles to link up with the very scenic Talyllyn Railway; or in the other direction there are all manner of destinations. The small, time-warped seaside resort of Barmouth (Abermaw) is one such stop travelling north – it still has donkeys strolling the enormous beach and colourful swingboats rocking back and forth.

Railway fans will love the miniature Fairbourne Railway, which chugs its way along the sand spit poking out into the Mawddach Estuary, to drop passengers off in front of one of the most ravishing views in

Britain. Once the Mawddach Estuary is seen, along with its encircling mountains, life is certain never to match up to its beauty in the same way again.

The Mawddach Trail, which follows the course of the disused railway from Morfa Mawddach, near Fairbourne, to Dolgellau, is one of the most enchanting walks (or bike rides) anywhere and, with the tide ebbing and flowing, the place never looks the same from one minute to the next.

Those mountains that overlook the

Mawddach on the south bank also come right down to the sea at Cae Du, and it won't be long before twitchy feet find their way on to the heights of Cader Idris.

And this is the thing – whatever you want to do with your camping break, it won't be far from Cae Du, even though it seems to be placed in another world.

THE UPSIDE Fantastic location directly next to the sea and a dishwashing view that might just inspire the undomesticated.

THE DOWNSIDE Can be a little exposed in angry weather and level ground hard to come by.

THE DAMAGE Tent and 2 adults £10, family £15 and single £6–10. Dogs on leads are welcome.

THE FACILITIES Excellent, with hot and cold water, toilets, showers, laundry, and dishwashing facilities, but no electric hook-ups. Wood for campfires, lamb burgers made at the farm and eggs (depending on how the hens are feeling) are sold at the farmhouse.

NEAREST DECENT PUB This isn't ideal pub-crawling territory, but 3 miles away at Bryncrug,

the Peniarth Arms (01654 711505) does decent pub grub. A few miles further towards Dolgellau, at Penmaenpool, the George III Hotel (01341 422525; www.georgethethird.co.uk) boasts a cosy bar, an exceptional restaurant and scenic location overlooking the Mawddach Estuary. It also has good rooms.

IF IT RAINS There are several train rides nearby; from Tonfanau station, 1 mile south of the campsite, the scenic Cambrian Coast service (08457 484950; www.traveline.org.uk) runs to Pwllheli in one direction and Shrewsbury in the other; the Fairbourne Railway (01341 250362; www.fairbournerailway.com) and the Talyllyn Railway (01654 710472; www.talyllyn.co.uk).

Or if it's really pouring, head to the little cinema in Tywyn (01654 710260) and catch a film.

GETTING THERE Take the M54/A5 to Shrewsbury, then the A458/A470 to Dolgellau and the A493 towards Tywyn. The site is 2½ miles beyond Llwyngwril.

PUBLIC TRANSPORT Take the coastal rail service to Tonfanau then hop into a taxi or brave the mile-long walk on foot.

OPEN Mar–Oct.

IF IT'S FULL Another good campsite in the area is at Garth Y Fog (07909 514669 or 01341 250254; www.snowdonialogcabins.co.uk) near Fairbourne, which overlooks the drama of the hills and the Mawddach Estuary.

Cae Du, Rhoslefain, Tywyn LL36 9ND

| | t | 01654 711234 | 36 | on the map |

bwlchgwyn farm

Bwlchgwyn Farm, which doubles up as a pony-trekking centre, is a fantastically located campsite clinging to the edge of Snowdonia National Park. Obviously this is a bonus for riders who don't have far to venture for a daily hack, but even without horses this unfussy campsite comes highly recommended. Stand at the top level and you've majestic panoramas of Fairbourne's long, sandy beach, the Mawddach Estuary and bustling Barmouth (Abermaw). If you tire of this picture-book scene (and you really won't), there's so much to do, right on your doorstep, that you'll have a truly action-packed holiday, should you want one.

Families love the two-mile Blue Flag sandy beach and the rockpools. Shallow tides here mean that the water's edge is just a short walk from wherever you throw down your towels, which the youngsters like.

Surfers love the tides that come swishing in and out of Tremadog Bay, further north, while equestrian fans soon make a beeline for Bwlchgwyn Farm's huge barn stable, from where the guided rides set out. The site is equally a winner among groups of friends; those breathtaking views from the top land open up an expansive, airy freedom that sets the perfect scene and pace for a memorable camping party.

As you inch up the drive of this working sheep and cattle farm it's impossible to ignore the unmistakable sounds and smells of the busy pony-trekking centre. Up to 30 Welsh cobs are lovingly tended to by local stable hands and their bosses, the campsite owners. Check in at reception, the farmhouse kitchen, and drive onwards – taking care not to run over any of the roaming sheep or chickens – up to the caravan park. Keep going to the next level and you'll see a line of motorhomes (also not a sight you'll find at most *Cool Camping* sites). Keep going, twisting around the hill to the left and up to the top. There all you have to do is angle your tent to keep the vehicles out of view, and be knocked out by the lovely coastal scenes.

With the Irish Sea to your left and Barmouth's seaside splendour perched on the opposite side of a broad expanse of estuary, criss-crossed by a rickety-looking wooden road bridge – this setting is a real treat. Kick back under the broad skies with a hot cup of tea in the morning or a cold, stronger something at sunset and fall in love with the bucolic charm of this idyllic setting.

There is a big 'but' to all this effusive praise. The facilities. For many farmers, opening up fields to campers is just a way of earning an extra income. Some may not

have yet stretched their budget to equip their guests with an all-singing, all-dancing shower and WC unit. Should their concrete shower block look too unappealing there's a mobile shower unit for campers. That, too, is nothing fancy, but it'll do. If you like to preen and gloss your body daily then perhaps just book in for a long weekend. However long you stay, a ride is a must. Sign up for the daily rides that wend slowly on to the beach. No experience is necessary; beginners can join the queue, while experienced riders can join the faster hacks.

Fairbourne village has all you need: post office, grocer, butcher and a fabulous Indian restaurant. It even has the Fairbourne Railway mini steam train shuttling people past Cardigan Bay beaches and the Mawddach Estuary, under the mountains of Snowdonia to Barmouth Ferry Station, from where you can catch a boat to Barmouth. If that's whetted your appetite for locomotive travel, then spend a day out on the Cambrian Railway and watch the stunning Welsh coastline unfold before you.

THE UPSIDE Beaches, horses, views – all on the edge of a national park. Privvy to west-coast-facing sunsets that rival any in New Zealand.
THE DOWNSIDE Manure on the drive might be offputting, but the paddock might be moved away from the campsite soon, so this is no biggie.
THE DAMAGE Two people with tent £12–16, £5 per extra adult, £3 per extra child (3–16). Five tourer pitches £15 per night, awnings £2, gazebos £4, £2 dogs (on a lead). Most caravans in the park are privately owned, but there are 3 available for rent, £100–500 per week.
THE FACILITIES A shabby concrete block by the caravan park has 6 loos and 2 showers (£1 for 10 minutes). The temporary unit on the touring field is heated with 2 showers, loos, sinks and urinals. Washing machine (£3.40) tumble-dryer (£1.70). Hook-ups £4 per night. Two-hour horse rides cost

£30 for novices and £37 for experienced riders.
NEAREST DECENT PUB The Last Inn at Barmouth (www.lastinn-barmouth.co.uk) is a 15th-century original turned gastro-pub, where you can watch the world go by from intimate outdoor tables set among potted flowers.
IF IT RAINS Have a day on the Cambrian Railway (08451 284680; www.westcoastrailways.co.uk). Otherwise, get noshing. The bijou Indiana Cuisine (3 Beach Road, Fairbourne; 01341 250891), run by a former Bollywood superstar Mayur Verma, is one hell of a tasty restaurant situated at the entrance of Fairbourne. Try the yellow lentils and coconut (locally reared) lamb.
GETTING THERE Bwlchgwyn Farm is located between the villages of Arthog and Fairbourne in the county of Gwynedd, north Wales. From the south east use the M40 or the M1 then take the

M6/M54/A5/A458 and A470 to the Dolgellau bypass. From the south west take the M5/M6, then as above. From the north take the M6/M56 to Chester, then the A494 to the Dolgellau bypass. From the Dolgellau bypass (A470) take the A493 coast road towards Tywyn and Fairbourne. Drive through the village of Arthog. The site is located on the left just before you reach Fairbourne.
PUBLIC TRANSPORT Trains run to Morfa Maddach (change at Machynlleth if coming from Birmingham or London) then the site owners can pick you up. Or take a train to Tywyn or Dolgellau, from where buses run past Fairbourne beach, stopping near the campsite.
OPEN Early Mar–late Oct.
IF IT'S FULL Another beautifully located coastal site in Mid-Wales is Cae Du (p185).

Bwlchgwyn Farm, Fairbourne, Gwynedd LL39 1BX

| t | 01341 250107 | w | www.bwlchgwynfarm.co.uk | 37 | on the map |

graig wen

Only mad dogs and Englishmen go out in the midday sun, right? Well, where does that leave the Welsh? As anyone who's done their research will know, even in high summer the weather can be unpredictable in Wales. But see the lush, green valleys (lush, meaning attractive, is a word the Welsh adore) all around you? Their stunning looks are thanks to the beauty regime of a wet climate. Of course, the sun does come out in Wales, often within an hour of rain, and there are days and days of dry spells. It's simply potluck as to when to expect continual blazing sunshine. Whatever the weather, this campsite will be an unmissable experience.

As one of the smartest operations in the book, everything the hosts do, they do to impress. Only two years ago the land was filled with old caravans, car batteries and monster conifers, so it's incredible that the new owners came along and won the Green Snowdonia Award in 2009 for Most Sustainable Campsite. John and Sarah's dedicated professionalism starts with a good-looking website. Well-maintained facilities with hot showers are kept spick and span. Viewing benches overlooking the Mawddach Estuary offer the best seat in the house at sunset o'clock. There are various regular events: you can sleep under the stars in hammocks, enrol in a fire-making

workshop or enlist in a wild-food weekend, eating only what you source outdoors (garlic pesto, and fish and nettle beer, for instance).

The pitches themselves are positioned to suit most tastes. Starting at the top: adjacent to the ranch-style B&B is space for 10 tourers or tents. A parallel track leads to two yurts, sleeping two and five. Isolated and sheltered among dense woodland, they offer total privacy. Back down the track you pass through a top gate and walk down a steep decline. Career off through the hedgerow, heather and bracken to two 'wild' camping spots that the owners hope will be a hit with backpackers and student types.

At the foot of the hill, the land opens up to 10 spacious, unmarked pitches for families. Tumbling seawards, the field unravels a few more secluded camping spots christened Monk's Corner, Precipice Pitch and Buzzard's Perch. The track ends at an open grassy area that would be good for groups (energetic ones, though – it's quite a walk to get anywhere the rest of the time). From the family camping field follow a footpath past a compost loo and down to the Lower Camping Field, where half-a-dozen pitches offer close-ups of the estuary. There's no noise or light pollution; nothing but a tranquil communion with nature. Warming yourself by a fire,

under a star-splattered night sky, you'll feel a million miles from home. From here, you've easy access to the Mawddach Trail, too.

Make the most of exploring every nook of this wonderful part of the world. Just across the road is the hilly climb to the two Cregennen Lakes that loom 250 metres above sea level under a sky mist, surrounded by heather and moorland. Travel back down for beautiful views before heading to Barmouth (Abermaw) via the rickety wooden bridge,

stopping at the charming George III Inn, grabbing an outside table and a tasty platter.

Intrepid explorers could tackle Cader Idris (Cadair Idris), the spectacular mountain right at the back of Graig Wen. It's a 10-minute drive to a cheap car park in a farmer's field, avoiding the crowds you get on the summit of Snowdon. And then there's the added challenge that, according to legend, if you spend the night on the top of Cader, you'll come down a poet or, yes, a madman...

THE UPSIDE Smooth access to walking, cycling, eating, sightseeing, swimming and 30 mins from Snowdonia by car.
THE DOWNSIDE Steep hill climbs to facilities, but it'll only make you fitter. For now, the lower camping fields open for just 4 weeks from the last week of July. Check the website for dates.
THE DAMAGE Touring site: £7 per adult and £3 for children under 16; under 5s and dogs on leads free. Tent camping fields: adults £7 per night Sun–Thur, £10 per night Fri and Sat. Under 16s £3 per night Sun–Thur and £5 per night Fri and Sat. Under 5s free, £1 for showers. B&B rooms cost from £70 for single occupancy to £120 for double en suite room with estuary view. Back/bikepackers less. Soul Pad bell tent £60 per night.
THE FACILITIES Twelve pitches at the top and 20–25 in the Lower Camping Fields. Two yurts, one sleeping 5 and one sleeping 2. Bell tent for hire in August. Two unisex showers, electric

hook-ups £3 per night. Campfires allowed on lower fields and communal campfire for touring site; bag of logs £5. Owners sell eggs, ice cream, marshmallows and breakfast hampers in high season (local bacon, sausages, bread, juice) for £18. Hire bikes at Dolgellau Cycles (01341 423332) for £20 for a full day.
NEAREST DECENT PUB The George III Hotel (Penmaenpool, Dolgellau, Gwynedd LL40 1YD, 01341 422525; www.georgethethird.co.uk) is a 2-hour walk away or 30 mins by bike. Locally produced lamb, beef and fish can be enjoyed outside in view of the estuary.
IF IT RAINS Check out the handcrafted furniture at the Corris Craft Centre (01654 761584) at Corris on the A487. There's also a selection of arts and crafts, including tables, glass works, quilts and jewellery.
GETTING THERE On the road between Dolgellau and Fairbourne. Turn off the A470 Dolgellau

bypass and take the A493 signposted Tywyn/ Fairbourne. A mile before Arthog village you'll spot a post box on your right, the site is 200 metres on from that on the right.
PUBLIC TRANSPORT Morfa Mawddach railway station, about 1½ miles from site, is accessible by foot/cyclepath or bus. Sarah and John encourage people to use public transport and will knock a small amount off the nightly bill if you don't come in a car. Buses run between Aberystwyth/ Machynlleth and Dolgellau. Ask the driver to drop you off at Graig Wen between Penmaenpool and Arthog. Traveline Cymru 0871 2002233.
OPEN Top field all year, Lower Camping Fields currently open end July–Aug. Check website for dates. The touring site at the top is open for small tents, vans and caravans pretty much all year (well, until 5 Jan).
IF IT'S FULL Magical Bwlchgwyn Farm (p191) is down the coast, with breathtaking sea views.

Graig Wen, Arthog, Nr Dolgellau, Gwynedd LL39 1BQ

| t | 01341 250482 | w | www.graigwen.co.uk | 38 | on the map |

YR YMDDIRIEDOLAETH
GENEDLAETHOL
THE NATIONAL TRUST
DWR YFED
DRINKING SUPPLY

DIM NOFIO
NO SWIMMING

owen tyddyn farm

A couple of million years ago, Cader Idris grew out of the greatest period of volcanicity that the earth had ever experienced and, although not a volcano itself, it has the same air of unpredictability and mystery about it. Cader Idris stands tall and proud, towering over the fields at its base. Against this awe-inspiring backdrop the sheep are like tiny white cotton balls in a patchwork of green grass and pink heather.

There are three main routes up Cader Idris, all of them arduous. The path from the Ty Nant Valley is the most popular from the Dolgellau side and is perhaps the easiest. It begins at the entrance to Ty Nant Farm as you leave the National Trust car park. As you begin your epic walk, you see the jagged ridge of Idris and the other peaks, namely Mynydd, Pen y Gader (the summit) and Cyfrwy (the saddle). On the hike up you pass picturesque landscapes of mirrored lakes, bare and forested peaks and rocky cairns, all coming to a perfect climax at the summit, nearly 915 metres into the heavens. On a clear day, the views – of what seems like the rest of Wales – are breathtaking.

At the foot of this mighty mountain is a campsite with front-seat views of Idris. Although not blessed with ideal facilities, the splendour of the setting more than makes up for this. This small farm is run by the friendly Owen Tyddyn with his two faithful dogs Alice and Mick. He drives around to collect camping fees on a battered old quad bike with his furry friends firmly ensconced on the back. He's always keen to stop for a chat about the weather, local legends – anything, really. He's obviously been in this remote, unpopulated spot a long, long time.

Farming has always been a vital part of the Snowdonia landscape and the whole national park that covers the area is, in fact, a collection of private farms, where families have lived for generations. Local authorities work closely with the park's community to lessen the impact of farming practices on the landscape. The aim is to enhance traditional features and support local communities – this means that there's a higher chance of creating all-important diversity.

Dolgellau used to be a famous market town, well known for its woollen cloth from the pedigree Welsh mountain sheep and the distinctive black cattle that were farmed here but, as Owen explains, it's virtually impossible to earn a living from cattle farming these days, hence his need to press one of his fields into service as a campsite. He has only a permit for a couple of caravans and a small number of tents, and one of the caravan pitches is occupied by an ageing contraption that has obviously been there a while. This caravan is owned by a couple in Birmingham who, when they first arrived, complained about the lambs munching the fixtures. Owen erected a fence and the couple have left their caravan here ever since – for the last 20 years!

The large sloping field is enclosed by dry-stone walls that stretch, seemingly endlessly, to the top of the mountain. The rest of the farm is covered in pink heather, which casts

a warm glow over the tents as the sun sets. Camping here can only be described as basic, but the breathtaking beauty and the clean mountain air make it special – along with the fact that campfires are permitted; welcome and useful to keep the evening chill at bay.

This site may not suit the first-time camper (or any camper in the middle of winter) but this is a great spot to dispense with the tent for a night, to sleep next to a fire under a blanket of sparkling stars and to wake to the magnificent site of Idris and a hot cup of tea.

THE UPSIDE Waking up to the breathtaking sight of Cader Idris.
THE DOWNSIDE No showers.
THE DAMAGE £5 per tent per night, including 2 people.
THE FACILITIES Two water points, chemical waste disposal, no showers. Toilets in National Trust car park (2-minute drive), mountain stream to wash in if you're brave. Campfires allowed.
NEAREST DECENT PUB A small local pub 1 mile down the road serves basic food, but only until 8.30pm. A better option is the pricier, but excellent, award-winning Welsh restaurant, Dylanwad Da (01341 422870; www.dylanwad. co.uk) in the town centre, which does superb

local lamb and steak dishes in the £15 range. For a really nearby option, just a ¼ mile away, the Gwesty Gwernan Hotel (01341 422488; www.gwernan.co.uk) has a cosy feel with an open log fire and does nice dinners.
IF IT RAINS Learn to ride a mountain bike with Snowbikers (01341 430628/07909 996983), hire one at MRX Bike Hire (01341 423008) and get on the superb tracks in nearby Coed y Brenin, the Mawddach Trail or Dyfi forest. Maps are available at Dolgellau Tourist Information office (01341 422888).
GETTING THERE Follow signs for Cader Idris through Dolgellau town centre. Turn right at the National Trust car park and follow the road, taking

the left fork, signposted 'Owen Tyddyn Camping'. Pass through another gate and the field is immediately on the left.
PUBLIC TRANSPORT Arriva and Trawscambria buses service this area (0870 6082608; www.trawscambria.info). The X94 goes between Barmouth and Wrexham via Dolgellau town centre.
OPEN Tents all year; caravans only for 28 days in Aug/Sept.
IF IT'S FULL Also boasting good access to Cader Idris, Hafod Dywyll (01341 423444) has 2 fields for camping, with the lower one next to a large stream. The facilities are basic, but they do have a shower and the best bit: proper campfires are allowed.

Owen Tyddyn Farm, Islawrdref, Dolgellau, Gwynedd LL40 1TL

| | t | 01341 422472 | 39 | on the map |

shell island

Shell Island is truly a camping phenomenon. Like the famous Fraser Island in Queensland, Australia, the whole place has been preserved in a wild and relatively undeveloped state and lucky campers can choose to pitch wherever they want over a whole 330 of its 460 acres.

It's not, strictly speaking, an island at all. It was – way back in the 19th century – but the vast sands of the beaches around the island began drifting, eventually forming huge sand dunes that now link it to the mainland. Despite this geographical quirk, its remoteness helps it to retain an islandy sort of feel, enhanced by the approach to the island across the two-mile St Patrick's Causeway, which disappears twice a day under the high tides.

The reality is that Shell Island isn't as idyllic as it should be – it has almost become a victim of its own popularity. On arrival, especially during peak times, it feels more like a downmarket holiday camp; signs bark instructions, sunburnt oiks and screaming kids spill out from the pub, shops and school-canteen-style snack bar, and it's a mad rush or a long queue to bag one of the busy showers. It may make you want to turn back, but that would mean missing out on a potentially first-class camping experience.

The trick is to successfully navigate the heaving reception area as speedily as humanly possible, then get the heck out of there. Flash your pass, through the barrier, up the hill past a row of tents – then it's down to you to find your very own slice of peninsula paradise.

And that's where Shell Island comes into its own. This large expanse of semi-wildness lets you find your own perfect pitch. Options include cliff-top spots with great views, sheltered fields near to the amenities or small enclaves hidden among the sand dunes, just a short scramble from the beach. There are a few highly sought-after pitches called 'the Hollows' down at shore level, right on the edge of the sea, or for real seclusion explore the woods at the eastward edge of the peninsula, where you'll find small, shady clearings among the trees.

Nowhere else in Wales gives you such freedom to camp wherever you like, over such a vast area, and with such a wide variety of sites – not to mention the chance to enjoy campfires. The simple, golden rule promoted by the Shell Island team is not to pitch within 20 metres of another tent. Add to this our own *Cool Camping* rule that you really need to arrive as early as possible to find a good pitch, especially during holidays

and summer weekends. If it's your first visit, it's well worth spending half an hour, or more, driving around the whole peninsula, exploring all the nooks and crannies and working out where you want to be. If it's really full, look for clues that people might be about to leave – a quick, polite chat is usually all that's required to confirm it and reserve a prime spot.

Just beyond the dunes, the beach stretches for more than six miles to the small seaside town of Barmouth (Abermaw). It's perfectly possible to walk there in about two hours at low tide, but do check the tide table first if you're planning a seaside stroll.

Given the beach, the remoteness and the spatial freedom that Shell Island gives you, it's not surprising that many families bag a good spot and stay here all summer. All over the island during July and August, you'll find mini-enclaves where multiple families have set up village-like settlements, marked out by colourful wind-breakers. They're hooked all right. Get past the madness that greets you at Shell Island's entrance, and you might soon be, too.

THE UPSIDE Remote, island-like camping.
THE DOWNSIDE Too many people in peak season. Try to come out of season or be prepared to spend a while finding a quiet corner.
THE DAMAGE Adults £6–7 a night, children £2.50. Weekly rates are available. Minimum 3 nights on Whitsun and August Bank Holiday. Tents and motorhomes only, no caravans. Dogs are allowed in some fields.
THE FACILITIES Supermarket, camping/beach shop, snack bar/restaurant, free hot showers, laundry and cheesy evening entertainment. For top-notch BBQ food, including delicious minted

Welsh spring lamb kebabs, head to Dylan Richards Family Butcher, in Llanbedr village, just over the causeway.
NEAREST DECENT PUB The onsite bar can get brash and noisy. For something more subdued, the Victoria Inn (01341 241213) is fashioned out of Welsh stone, has a steadfastly traditional interior and pretty beer garden. Bar food is served daily. It's almost opposite the entrance to the causeway back on the mainland.
IF IT RAINS It's only 3 miles to Harlech Castle (01766 780552; www.harlech.com), an impressive 13th-century fortress and a World Heritage Site.

GETTING THERE From Barmouth, take the A496 north towards Harlech. At Llanbedr village, turn left at the bridge and follow the road to the causeway.
PUBLIC TRANSPORT Llanbedr railway station on the Cambrian Coast line is on the mainland side of the causeway. It's a couple of miles to walk from there but feels longer if you are hauling heavy gear.
OPEN Mar–Oct.
IF IT'S FULL Just 2 miles inland from Llanbedr is the lovely countryside campsite of Dinas Farm (01341 241585; www.dinas-farm.co.uk) – ideal for walkers heading out into Snowdonia.

Shell Island, Llanbedr, Gwynedd LL45 2PJ

| | t | 01341 241453 | w | www.shellisland.co.uk | 40 on the map |

bwch-yn-uchaf

At the top of Lake Bala (Llyn Tegid) begins a magical journey into a rich historical and cultural past. Whether by train, by car or foot, the way winds alongside the banks of this top-notch lake, the largest freshwater expanse in Wales. It continues through fresh, green rolling hills, framed by the three massive peaks of Benllyn, Arenig and Fawr.

Because of its situation, set among the windy hills, the lake is perfect for windsurfing and sailing. No powerboats are allowed, but you can hire canoes, dinghies and windsurfboards. There are various slipways and launching places around the lake, but the main hub of activity is on the foreshore in front of the warden's office, where you can get the permits you need.

The bustling one-street market town of Bala (Y Bala), at the northern end of the lake, is a stronghold of the ancient Welsh language. With more than 80 per cent of the population speaking the region's mother tongue, it's useful to have a suitable local greeting or two up one's sleeve. It's a deeply traditional Welsh town – the harp is still taught at schools as part of the curriculum – and this area is a great place to catch a male voice choir at a rehearsal or performance. Try the village hall at Llanuwchllyn (at the other end of the lake to Bala) on Monday and Thursday nights or keep your ear to the ground – provided you understand Welsh.

Seldom out of sight of the lake throughout its four-mile journey is a narrow-gauge railway line operated by three steam locomotives. It begins its journey at Llanuwchllyn, on the outskirts of the Snowdonia National Park and, hugging the shoreline, makes its way to Bala. After the return journey, a visit to the signal box is an interesting diversion, where the stationmaster will demonstrate the original 1896 levers and lamps; an archaic confusion of wooden handles and outdated widgets.

The Rheilffors Llyn Tegid Cyf (Bala Lake Railway) is run almost entirely by volunteers and they're always on the lookout for willing helpers. So, if you've ever fancied driving a steam train or just blowing the whistle and waving the flag, become a member and live out your childhood dreams.

To the left of this quaint old railway station is the unpronounceable Bwch-yn-uchaf campsite. It begins with a vast field of mown lawn, which is great for those who want to pitch large tents and caravans. From here, there is a small drivable path that leads away from the main field and ablutions, and snakes its way through two smaller enclaves of grass, bordered by a tree-lined shallow river, which is just perfect for a spot of fishing or canoeing.

The narrow strip of riverside turf means that each pitch has an unobstructed view of the sparklingly clear river. The site is also backed by green banks and views of rolling hills, so you really feel like you are in the middle of rural Wales surrounded by peace, tranquillity and some slightly noisy sheep. There are portaloos and various water points in the middle of the three fields, which is handy if you don't feel like the longish, but

scenic, walk to the main ablution block. This is a dream-come-true location for every kid as they can play Pooh Sticks or skim pebbles across the river all day long. And when they tire of these activities, they can hang out at the station, watching the driver shovel coal into the engine and waving the day visitors on their way.

So, whether it's sailing on the lake, going walking in the mountains or simply having a bit of R&R in a valley with a steaming good view, this peaceful spot definitely has all the bases covered.

THE UPSIDE Narrow-gauge steam railway station, views, riverside setting.
THE DOWNSIDE Midges can be a problem in summer. Long walk to the main ablution block.
THE DAMAGE £11 for 2 people plus tent per night; children (4–15 years) £3, under 3 years free; dogs £1.50.
THE FACILITIES The facilities block has been extended so the campsite now boasts 7 toilets, 5 showers (hot water available all day), washing machine and tumble-dryer on coin meters, 3 washing-up sinks, electric plugs for hairdryers and an ice-pack freezing facility (no charge). There's also a disabled/family room and portaloos are located midway between the camping fields. Ten electric hook-ups and water points and

recycling bins are scattered around the site.
NEAREST DECENT PUB The Eagle Inn (01678 540278; www.theeagleinn-bala.co.uk), ½ mile away in Llanuwchllyn, is where the locals eat – and all the campers, too, if it's raining! Big portions of home-cooked food are on offer, including fish specialities and tasty wild boar sausages. There's also a beer garden with views.
IF IT RAINS Bala Lake Railway (01678 540666; www.bala-lake-railway.co.uk) makes a great outing, while Bala Watersports Centre (01678 521059; www.balawatersports.com) has all kinds of watercraft available for hire. Canolfan Tryweryn (01678 521083) offers white-water rafting or check out the brilliantly named sheep-themed attraction Ewe-phoria (01490 460369) for sheep shearing,

lamb-feeding and sheepdog demonstration (on sunnier days you can hire quad bikes there, too – www.adventure-mountain.co.uk).
GETTING THERE Take the A494 from Bala to Dolgellau, turn into Llanuwchllyn village, then follow signs to Bala Lake Railway. The campsite is next to the station.
PUBLIC TRANSPORT The steam train runs between the campsite and Bala; Trawscambria (0870 6082608; www.trawscambria.info) bus no X94 runs between Bala and Dolgellau and stops in Llanuwchllyn village, an easy walk to the campsite.
OPEN Mid Mar–late Oct.
IF IT'S FULL Two options, one either side of the lake, the less holiday-parkish of the two being Pant yr Omen (01678 520415).

Bwch-yn-uchaf, Llanuwchllyn, Bala, Gwynedd LL23 7DD

| | t | 01978 812179 | w | www.bwch-yn-uchaf.co.uk | 41 | on the map |

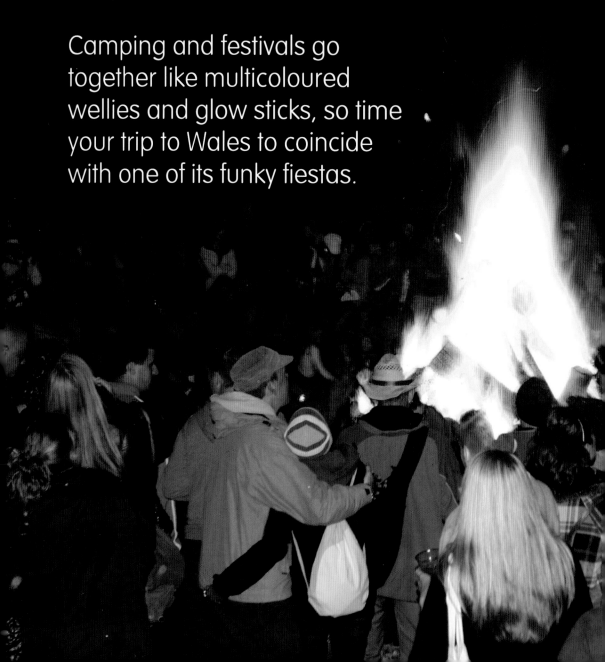

festival fun

Camping and festivals go together like multicoloured wellies and glow sticks, so time your trip to Wales to coincide with one of its funky fiestas.

What's a summer without a festival to get well and truly immersed in? Now a huge part of our Great British culture, festivals have been springing up here, there and everywhere, in all kinds of different shapes and sizes. They offer us the chance to kiss goodbye to the daily grind and let our hair down good and proper.

Whether it's the muddy great fun to be had at the big daddy of UK festivals, Glastonbury, or the tiny peaceful affairs of the boutique festivals; from kid-centric bashes to hedonistic benders; cultural dos to hippified-folk gatherings, the UK just loves its festivals and there's one out there to suit just about everyone and cater for just about every taste. Wales hosts its fair share of them – dotted about the country in some of the most spectacular settings known to festivals.

So, whether you're a foodie with a hunger for a whole festival dedicated to the digestible, a culture vulture keen on book fests, a party animal aching for an action-packed mêlée, a straightforward music-lover or just want to make the most of a weekend, without further ado, we'd like to introduce you to a few Welsh bashes that are really too good to be missed.

Music: Green Man

Set against the awe-inspiring Black Mountains and sitting within a perfect green bowl of land, Green Man Festival has a suitably mystical stage from which to belt out all sorts of guitar-led folk and rock beats. The crowd comprises one good-humoured mass of up to 10,000 festivalees. Kids' activities abound, so it's a firm festival fave among families, and foodies can treat their taste buds to a ravishing by the world food on offer (like Goan fish curry, to name but one). This chilled-out affair culminates in a blaze of glory when the huge bark and wood Green Man is set alight and revellers make merry around the gigantic bonfire.

Glanusk Park Estate, Crickhowell, Powys NP8 1LP
www.thegreenmanfestival.co.uk; August

Food: Abergavenny Food Festival

Every year this picturesque little town hosts a food-lover's idea of paradise. Stalls spill on to the cobbled streets, all offering gastronomic delights produced, grown or reared in Wales. TV-favourite chefs like Hugh Fearnley-Whittingstall, Antony Worrall Thompson and Clarissa Dickson Wright (do all good chefs need to have so many names?) have been known to make appearances, and cookery demos, master classes and tastings abound. Fresh produce is championed and we defy anyone to walk away without an edible souvenir in their bag-for-life. On the Saturday night there's a huge party at the castle to burn off some of those calories.

Abergavenny, Monmouthshire
www.abergavennyfoodfestival.com; September

Action/Music: Wakestock

This huge North-Walian party combines the music and good times of a festival with a big burst of action-fuelled adrenalin courtesy of a wakeboarding competition. Running for over 10 years now, Wakestock knows how to draw the crowds and provide them with the best of summer-party atmospheres. During the days spectators cluster at the Pwllheli marina to watch the world's best compete using speedboat wakes to perform incredible stunts and skeleton-defying shapes. Then audiences head to the festival's stages to hear and get on down to big names such as Calvin Harris, Noisettes, NERD, Dizzee Rascal, the Zutons and Moby.

Pen-y-Berth, Penrhos, Pwllheli, Gwynedd LL53 7HG
www.wakestock.co.uk; July

Culture: Hay Literary Festival

Whether you're a fully fledged bookworm or have hardly any interest in the written word (but as you're reading this, we'll take it that you do…) the Hay Literary Festival is worth a visit, if only to soak up the rich cultural atmosphere. A day here will leave you feeling your IQ has shot up a couple of points and you're ready for a little intellectual sparring with the likes of Stephen Fry and David Starkey. The 10-day programme is varied, with comedians and bands interspersed with lectures and literary talks. And the town itself (a mile or so from the festival site) is scrumptious, with second-hand book shops, cafés and antique shops galore.

Dairy Meadows, Brecon Road, Hay-on-Wye, Herefordshire HR3 5PJ; www.hayfestival.com; May

219

rynys farm

Decisions, decisions, decisions. Everywhere you turn there are choices to be made, people pressing you for an answer, offering you options: three dozen digital TV channels; a thousand mobile phone tariffs; tracker, fixed-rate and floating mortgages; the bargain bucket or the supersize with fizzy and fries? Press the red button now. Please hold while we try to connect you. Your call is important to us…

Rynys Farm is a no-nonsense campsite run by Carol Williams, a no-nonsense woman, who gives you two choices. Do you want to pitch in the upper field (spectacular but windy) or the lower field (spacious and secluded)? Simple, done, enjoy your stay.

The site is on a working farm nestled in the cleft of a soft, green hill above the town of Betws-y-Coed to the west of the mighty Snowdon, whose top can be seen from a knobble of rock in the lower field. The views are the kind you get in ads for fabric softener: gentle, soft and comforting. But then the odd tractor and bleating sheep remind you that this isn't an advertiser's stage set but real, live countryside.

The site's handy for the tourist hub of Snowdonia, the town of Betws-y-Coed. It's great if you like craft shops, outdoor wear and ice cream and was probably a real gem before the invention of the internal combustion engine. Now it suffers from having the A5 and its 18-wheelers rumbling through the middle of town. Still, it's a good base from which to explore the surrounding area and great for a cuppa if it rains. Try the Bistro up by the Spar, though the Conwy Falls Café at the foot of the road up to the site is equally good. They do things with eggs in the morning and for lunch put things between ciabatta.

As attractions go, the birthplace of the first man to translate the Bible into Welsh might not rank all that highly on your list. But old Bishop William Morgan's house at Ty Mawr Wybrnant, restored to its 16th-century glory, is a bit of a treasure trove of rural Welsh life. And even if you don't fancy going in, there's an adventure to be had just getting there. It's set in the southern part of the Gwydyr Forest Park and has a single-track road leading to it from Penmachno.

If you pass by the Bishop's House and carry on, through a gate, the road sprouts a thin Brazilian of grass, which grows ever more unkempt, until you're driving on little more than two ruts on either side of shin-high grass that tickles the underside of your car. Then the bracken closes in and the tarmac breaks up and you're into the real wild stuff. It's not for the fainthearted, but if you keep at it the road eventually brings you back out by Conwy Falls. And if it's too hairy to do by car, it makes a great semi-offroad bike trail.

For a more sedate time, Rynys Farm is plenty big enough to spread out and relax in. The upper field is the smaller area, with southerly valley views, while the lower field is more spacious and extends down the hill, bounded by an old stone wall and a stream.

Both fields catch the morning rays, bask in the warmth (with occasional showers), during the day and, as evening sets in, are raked by the sun setting slowly somewhere by Snowdon. It's all pretty simple, really, and the last decision of the day is only whether you'll want to stay here again tomorrow.

THE UPSIDE Above the tourist fray with fabric-softener views.

THE DOWNSIDE Occasional road noise. There's also one static caravan right between the 2 fields.

THE DAMAGE Adults are £6 and children are £2.50 per night. It's £2 for a caravan and a dog is 50p (and has to be kept on a lead).

THE FACILITIES An old stone building above the lower field has the WCs and showers (2 of each) and a kitchen and washing room. By the upper field there's a male and female WC. It's all kept clean and tidy, but the hot showers are 10p for 2 minutes or £3 an hour if you've had a hard day.

NEAREST DECENT PUB The locals' local is the White Horse in Capel Garmon (01690 710271). It's right opposite the village graveyard, which has fine views of Snowdon from between the gravestones.

IF IT RAINS This part of Wales is criss-crossed by little steam railways. There's the famous one up to the top of Snowdon (0871 7200033; www.snowdonrailway.co.uk) or a kiddies' one running out of Betws-y-Coed railway station. From Ffestiniog to Porthmadog there's the Ffestiniog Railway or from Porthmadog to Caernarfon there's the Welsh Highland Railway (details of both at 01766 516024; www.festrail.co.uk).

GETTING THERE A few miles short of Betws-y-Coed, past Rhydlanfair on the A5, as the road goes downhill and round a right-hand bend, there's a sign 50 metres before the campsite. Turn right and follow the road up a steep single-track road and, hey presto! From Betws-y-Coed, the entrance is just 50 metres past the Conwy Falls Café.

PUBLIC TRANSPORT There are reasonably frequent trains to Betws-y-Coed and the Llangollen bus service stops near the Conwy Falls Café, from which it's a steep walk up to the site.

OPEN The site is open for tents all year, but caravans and camper vans are allowed only between Easter and October.

IF IT'S FULL There's Tan Aeldroch Farm about 5 miles away on the A470 (p225) or alternatively back east along the A5 towards Pentrefoelas there's the Llwyn Onn Guesthouse (www.llwynonnguesthouse.co.uk), which has a small camping area out the back (though it is right next to the road).

Rynys Farm, Nr Betws-y-Coed, Gwynedd LL26 0RU					
	t	01690 710218	w	www.rynys-camping.co.uk	42 on the map

tan aeldroch farm

Say what you like about sheep – that they're not very bright and are too into their looks – but they do a great job of keeping the grass tidy. The campsite at Tan Aeldroch, a few miles along the River Lledr from Betws-y-Coed in Snowdonia, doubles as a sheep-grazing field so the grass is always well-kempt and the field rings to the bleats and baas of woolly grasscutters.

There is, though, as you might guess, a downside. Suffice to say it's small and brown and dotted around the site. Still, if you want to enjoy nature you have to take the rough with the smooth.

Tan Aeldroch is as close to wild camping as you can get within a stone's throw of an A road. It's a large riverside meadow accessed across a bridge, a bit marshy in places and surrounded by hand-built stone walls.

For quiz buffs, the bridge that crosses the River Lledr from the main road to the site once doubled as the Czech-Austrian border in the fifties' TV series *Danger Man*. The series was partly written by Ian Fleming and starred Patrick McGoohan, who went on to become *The Prisoner*, which was filmed at nearby Portmeirion. Now won't your summer evenings just fly by with trivia like this at your fingertips? It'll keep the kids' minds

off the fact that the site's a bit Ray Mears-y. It only has a couple of flush loos and a standpipe for facilities. But the upside is you can build your own fire in one of the fire pits arranged around the site.

Anyway, given that you're in the heart of the Snowdonia National Park, there's no point lounging around with the sheep. Swing round through Betws-y-Coed and Capel Curig and head up the Llanberis Pass to Snowdon (Yr Wyddfa) itself. There's always the famous cog railway that'll haul you up the mountainside if you can't face the climb.

In recent years the dreaded café at the top has been made a little more aesthetic and less of an affront to the great outdoors. At a cost of £8.5 million, the Hafod Eryri Visitor Centre is now worth the trip up in itself. Made largely of local slate and panelled in Welsh oak, it has a fantastic panoramic window, which means you can enjoy the views without getting a faceful of nasty weather. It's apt, really, that Hafod Eryri means 'summer shelter' in Welsh. Much of the time you need it.

If uphill isn't your style, there's the more sedate option of walking a section of the Sarn Helen, believed to be an old Roman road running from Aberconwy down to

Carmarthen (Caerfyrddin). It's now part of a mountain-biking trail that leads all the way to the Gower Peninsula. You probably won't want to walk all that, so pick it up at Pont-y-Pant and follow it across the hills and into Betws-y-Coed. Check out the Long Distance Walkers' Association website for details at www.ldwa.org.uk.

If even that seems too much, there's always a visit to Dolwyddelan Castle, a few miles along the road to the west. This hilltop keep guarded the Conwy Valley and the mountain pass in the 13th century, when Edward I was showing an unhealthy interest in Wales.

It's still an imposing site today, but instead of bearded Welsh warriors the site is now guarded by the ubiquitous sheep, tending to the grass and generally lounging around. How much good they'd be at repelling invaders is anyone's guess, but at least they keep the grass neat.

THE UPSIDE Riverside camping, with sheep as your neighbours.

THE DOWNSIDE The indiscriminate toiletry habits of the sheep.

THE DAMAGE Flat fee of £4.50 per night.

THE FACILITIES Rural. There's an old stone barn with a couple of flush loos apiece for ladies and gents. Oh, and a drinking water pipe. That's it.

NEAREST DECENT PUB The Y Gwydyr (01690 750209) is the only *gwy* in the village of Dolwyddelan, a mile or so west of the site. It's 'traditional'.

IF IT RAINS Nip up the road to the T Gwyn, a traditional coaching inn on the south side of the A5/A470 junction. The bar's a great place to while away a couple of hours over a pint and a game of 'Name That Raindrop'.

GETTING THERE Take the A470 from Betws-y-Coed towards Blaenau Ffestiniog. The site is about a mile and a half along the road, signposted on the left. Take the turning and follow the road down the hill and across the bridge. The site is on the left, but you'll need to go and say hello at the farmhouse on the right.

PUBLIC TRANSPORT Catch a branch-line train to Pont-y-Pant and from there it's a mile's walk back along the road to the site. There are buses running along the A470 between Betws-y-Coed and Blaenau Ffestiniog (number X1) but there's no official stop near the campsite. Speak nicely to the driver, though, and you might get let off.

OPEN Apr–Sept.

IF IT'S FULL Rynys Farm (p221) is 5 miles back east along the A5, or you can try Dol-Gam on the A5 west of Betws-y-Coed (01690 720228; www.dolgam-snowdonia.co.uk). It's a flat meadow site with views up to Snowdon (though it is right by the main road).

Tan Aeldroch Farm, Pont-y-Pant, Dolwyddelan, Conwy LL25 0LZ		
	t 0151 7287639	43 on the map

gwern gôf isaf farm

Gwern Gôf Isaf is more a place of legend than a mere campsite, where generations of mountaineers have come to challenge themselves on the steep crag-ringed slopes of perhaps the most impressive hill in Wales – the mighty Tryfan.

At one time, not so many years ago, the Williams family, who have been running a campsite here now for several generations, would welcome just the committed hill folk, who were hell-bent on standing atop the Tryfan's 900-metre-high pinnacles. But, in recent years, a wider audience have pitched their tents here, if just to be in the presence of this startling scenery without necessarily intending to trample all over it. But not many leave without either climbing the mountain or promising themselves that one day they will stand on top of Tryfan.

If you are coming here for the hill-walking, then it really doesn't get any better, with not only Tryfan to keep your feet (and hands) busy, but also the amazing Glyder Ridge, semi-detached to the back of Tryfan and, across the other side of the valley, the Carneddau, which are, in terms of bulk, the biggest range of hills in Snowdonia.

When the mountains overlooking the site have been conquered, it is but a short drive to Pen-y-Pass, from where the biggest Welsh pile of them all, Snowdon (or to be precise Yr Wyddfa) can be tackled. The scariest route up is via the Crib Goch Ridge and be in no doubt about this – it is very exposed.

The most scenic clamber is the Miners' Track, while the easiest way of walking to the top of Snowdon is via the Pyg Track. There is another, less-energetic option though; get yourself to Llanberis and pay the not inconsiderable cost of a ticket for the Snowdon Mountain Railway. There are those who consider this means of getting astride Snowdon to be even scarier than the Crib Goch route. And, it has to be said, it's a terrifying experience for the wallet, too.

Also at Llanberis is the National Slate Museum (p149), which paints a very bleak, but compelling, picture of life in the huge quarries that were the lifeblood of this area in Victorian times, and an even bleaker picture of life when they became uneconomic in the last century.

If clambering up big, steep, dangerous mountains isn't your principal interest in the scenery then there is a good variety of less challenging things to do and places to visit. A walk along Bangor Pier is one, for a lovely panoramic view back at the hills;

and nearby Penrhyn Castle, previous home of one of the former slate barons, gives a spectacular, but slightly sickening, insight into the inequalities of Victorian society. Bodnant Garden (home of yet another slate baron), near Conwy, is one of the most beautiful gardens in the world, and the Llechwedd Slate Caverns are an amazing and emotional glimpse into how the quarries actually functioned.

If you love to cycle, take advantage of the site's location on the Sustrans National Cycle Route 8 between Tryfan and Bangor. A couple of miles from the campsite the National Mountain Centre, Plas y Brenin (01690 720214) offers short courses in canoeing, orienteering, climbing and abseiling.

Gwern Gôf Isaf may very well be a place of mountaineering legends, but it allows everybody to get a taste of it, or for it, but not to have to entirely swallow it. Most of all, though, the scenery outside your tent is absolutely awesome.

THE UPSIDE Amazing vertical, rocky scenery all around and a whole gamut of challenging walks on to it.
THE DOWNSIDE Pesky midges often like to dine on campers here and in the rain the ground can get squishy. Your furry sidekicks will have to stay at home as dogs aren't allowed onsite.
THE DAMAGE Adults £4, children £2 and babies/toddlers free. Tents and small motorhomes only; if you have a touring caravan please call ahead to check.
THE FACILITIES The facilities block was upgraded in 2008 and is now equipped with 5 toilets, 3 showers and washing-up sinks.

There's also chemical toilet disposal and electric hook-ups.
NEAREST DECENT PUB The nearest pubs are in Bethesda, some 7 miles away, and 2 hotels just beyond Capel Curig in the other direction some 3½ miles from the site. The pick of them is the Cobdens Hotel in Capel Curig (01690 720243; www.cobdens.co.uk), where they do their own beer and specialise in cooking the local animal life, such as rabbits and lambs.
IF IT RAINS A whole, ahem, slate of options including Llechwedd Slate Caverns (01766 830306; www.llechwedd-slate-caverns.co.uk) at Blaenau Ffestiniog; Sygun Copper Mine (01766

890595; www.syguncoppermine.co.uk); and Penrhyn Castle (01248 371337; www.nationaltrust.org.uk).
GETTING THERE From the south and Midlands follow the A5 from the M54, all the way to the site. From the north take the A55, then the A5 through Bethesda to the campsite.
PUBLIC TRANSPORT Catch the train to Bangor, then hop on a local bus to Capel Curig, which goes directly past the site.
OPEN All year.
IF IT'S FULL Other good camping sites nearby include the spectacularly landscaped (but popular) Conwy Touring Park (01492 592856).

Gwern Gôf Isaf Farm, Capel Curig, Betws-y-Coed, Conwy LL24 0EU

| t | 01690 720276 | w | www.gwerngofisaf.co.uk | 44 on the map |

llyn gwynant

Something about Llyn Gwynant needs to be explained right from the start – it can be a bit of a madhouse at times. Well, perhaps madhouse isn't quite the right word – though neither is it that wrong either. This large campsite can accommodate one hell of a lot of campers and quite often that is exactly how many can be found here. But it's only really a madhouse because everybody seems to be busy doing something, or about to do something, or planning to do something, or recovering from just having done something – such is the variety of activities either in progress on the site, next to it, leaving from it, or just coming back from it. 'Frenetic' may be more accurate. 'Hyperactive' may be going just a little too far, but by now the message must be sinking in: if you want outdoor action combined with your camping then Llyn Gwynant is probably *the* place to come to.

The list of activities taking place on, near, or from, the site on the late May Bank Holiday weekend, when the *Cool Camping* crew pitched up, reads as follows: canoeing, sailing, rafting, walking, rock-climbing, abseiling, boateering, gorge-scrambling and the presently trendy activity of coasteering. Not to mention just sitting there, wide-eyed, watching it all happen. With all this lot going on and the waters of Llyn Gwynant

so handy for just messing about in, an active family holiday takes on a whole new meaning here, offering an opportunity for everyone to get completely cream-crackered by the end of the day.

The variety and scale of the attractions on offer at Llyn Gwynant during school holidays does mean that a large number of young folk of all ages are actively encouraged to come here – and you'd think that this would create a noise problem occasionally wouldn't you? Well, possibly, but with careful proactive management, in all the years the site has been operating the incidence of noisy or unruly behaviour has been almost non-existent.

All those who love campfires can indulge themselves at Llyn Gwynant with 250 fire grates provided free for campers' use. All that they ask is that only wood purchased onsite is used, and that you don't take it home with you, of course.

While Llyn Gwynant is probably the top campsite in Britain for an activity-based family holiday, everything changes when the little darlings are installed back in their institutions. This is when Llyn Gwynant truly becomes itself, and it's then that this staggeringly scenic campsite transforms itself into one of the best places in Britain for the more reclusive camper: the kind of camper who just wants to immerse themselves in the natural beauty right in the heart of Snowdonia, or bring the tent for a few days of peak-bagging in the surrounding mountains, or just lazily paddle about untroubled in the crystal-clear waters of Llyn Gwynant.

With Llyn Gwynant's host of outdoor activities and all that scenery just begging to be enjoyed, it would be easy to forget that Snowdonia has quite an array of tourist attractions for whiling away wetter days,

and this campsite's location makes them all easily accessible. Indeed, if you really want to stand out from the macho crowd, there is even a railway which clutches and crawls its way to the top of Snowdon from Llanberis, just over the hill. However, *Cool Camping*'s man on the spot reckons walking up (and especially down) is the less scary option.

So which Llyn Gwynant do you want to camp at? The mad, frantic outdoor activity-led campsite during the school holidays, or that peaceful near-empty hideaway in the mountains? It's just a matter of timing.

THE UPSIDE Scenic location and a staggering array of outdoor activities on offer during the school holidays. Superb place to walk or canoe from. Huge site (441 pitches) with no booking in advance. Very carefully managed to avoid nuisance or noise.

THE DOWNSIDE Not the place for some at peak periods. The 'no advance bookings' policy for pre-booked holiday periods. Occasionally the midges can be a real pain here.

THE DAMAGE Adults £8 per night high season, £6 low season; children (5–15 years) £4; dogs £1; firewood £4 per bag; refundable noise bond of £20 per person for non-family groups.

THE FACILITIES Modern, well-maintained block with toilets, showers, and new laundry for 2010.

NEAREST DECENT PUB The Pen-Y-Gwryd

Hotel (01286 870211; www.pyg.co.uk) is 2 miles away along an old Roman road, and is where the 1953 Everest team stayed while training, so is now the haunt of hill folk. Traditional atmosphere and excellent food.

IF IT RAINS Bodnant Gardens (01492 650460; www.bodnantgarden.co.uk) near Conwy is especially stunning in late May or early June while Welsh Mountain Zoo (01492 532938; www.welshmountainzoo.org), near Colwyn Bay, is well worth a visit. Penrhyn Castle (01248 371337; www.nationaltrust.org.uk), Bangor, is decadence on a huge scale. Welsh Highland Railway (01766 51600; www.welshhighlandrailway.net) from Caernarfon to Portmadog. Conwy Castle (01492 592358; www.conwy.com), Conwy. Great place when taken with the old town walls. Caernarfon

Castle (01286 677617; www.caernarfon.com) is the archetypal ruin. Snowdon Mountain Railway (0844 4938120; www.snowdonrailway.co.uk), Llanberis.

GETTING THERE Follow the A5 from Betws-y-Coed to Capel Curig, turn left along the A4086 for 5 miles, to Pen-y-Gwryd, then take the A498 for 2½ miles and the site is on the right.

PUBLIC TRANSPORT A regular bus service passes the site to Caernarfon and Beddgelert.

OPEN Week before Easter–mid Nov.

IF IT'S FULL One nearby site is Snowdonia Parc, or, nearer still, with good facilities, is Cae Du (not the Cae Du on p185) 4 miles away near Beddgelert (01766 890345; www.caeducampsite.co.uk).

Llyn Gwynant, Nantgwynant, Gwynedd LL55 4NW

| | t | 01766 890340 | w | www.gwynant.co.uk | 45 | on the map |

aberafon

Let us not beat about the bush here – this campsite scores on the old 'location, location, location' chestnut. Or should that be 'situation, situation, situation'? The location of Aberafon is about 10 miles south of Caernarfon, just off the main road (the A499) into the Llyn Peninsula or, more locally, some two miles north of the small village of Trefor, at the bottom of a narrow lane heading west.

Nothing remarkable, maybe, but the situation is astonishing. However, while negotiating the steep, narrow, tortuous lane to the site, and even while booking in at the farmhouse, there isn't really any hint of the sublime situation; though there is a feeling that you are in a secret valley within the mountains. A joyful tumbling stream burbles past the amenities block and also by the first little clearing, where a few tents are idyllically pitched. You can even see the tops of some rather big hills looming large over the site.

So the situation of Aberafon is that of a small site located in a beautiful, secretive mountain setting surrounded by big, bold scenery. Well, yes, but that's only half of the astonishing situation, as you are about to discover as you walk (pedal, drive or whatever) on to the main part of the site, which is a hundred paces further west.

There are several small(ish) fields available for campers and, while this may not sound exciting thus far, they all have one thing in common: a very abrupt ending – where they meet the sea. And a stunning view taking in the hills behind, along with the relentless ocean attempting to wash them away.

The stunning view here is much more than just nice to have about, though, or for merely fixing your karma after a hard day out sightseeing (or walking or cycling or canoeing). For that rugged and wild meeting place of land and water is immediately accessible from the site and only from the site, making this, in effect, a private beach.

Initially, the beach does look just a tad too rugged to be useful, but a stroll along the shore shows that this is a great place to let the children (aged 5–95) loose for traditional seaside pleasures. *Cool Camping*'s team of (not so) intrepid explorers walked miles along the shore from Aberafon and we can confidently state that there is much more here to hold the gaze than a mere sandy beach. One of the team even went for a swim and found the water just a bit too invigorating (in early May), but easy enough to get in and out of. Children were acquainting themselves with the rockpools, wearing lengths of kelp as scarves, carrying buckets of crabs and generally getting to know the seaside without meddling parents getting in the way. There is also a bit of sand for castellated constructional purposes, but there were just too many other interesting things to poke at or pick up for sculpting the sand to be a priority.

The usefulness of the seaside doesn't end there, either, as there is also a slipway to launch your boat from, if you carry one with you. Be it canoe or dinghy, skiff or speedboat. Those of you with an eye on the scenery can't help but notice how much there is hereabouts and the most noticeable nearest chunk, Yr Eifl, is also one of the most intriguing to put under the boots.

All sorts of other walking opportunities are available nearby, as are the many and varied tourist attractions of Snowdonia and the Llyn Peninsula. So how best to describe the charm of Aberafon? Great location? Superb situation? Or how about astonishing situation in a great location?

THE UPSIDE Fantastic isolated seaside situation, where children can enjoy real independence and explore their surroundings. Wonderful scenery. Getting-away-from-it-all for families.
THE DOWNSIDE Awkward access; the ground can get a bit moist after heavy rain and the isolated nature of the place may be a little too removed for some, with the nearest supermarket in Caernarfon, combined with the fact that the onsite shop is only open in school holidays. Fires allowed only on the beach.
THE DAMAGE Adults £6.50; children £2.75; dogs £1.50; electric hook-up £2.95; boat (on trailer) £3; showers 20p.
THE FACILITIES A bit rambling and scattered; not the newest or most luxurious, but clean and tidy, including toilets, showers, laundry, dishwashing, electric hook-ups to some pitches,

television and games room, and that stunning sea view from most pitches. Onsite shop supplies daily essentials.
NEAREST DECENT PUB There is only one for miles about – Y Beuno (01286 660785) – which is about 1½ miles away. The food is good and caters for all tastes and is a proper 'local' rather than a trendy tourist haunt.
IF IT RAINS There are all sorts happening nearby, including the historic and rather quaint little town of Caernarfon, with its awesome castle (01286 677617; www.caernarfon-castle.co.uk), the Welsh Highland Railway steams from Caernarfon (01776 51600; www.welshhighlandrailway.net) all the way to Porthmadog through the mountains. The atmospheric Llechwedd Slate Caverns (01766 830306; www.llechwedd-slate-caverns.co.uk) are a must-see, while Penrhyn Castle at Bangor (01248

371337; www.nationaltrust.org.uk) is decadence on a massive scale. A bit nearer is the eccentric Caernarfon Airworld Museum (01286 830800; www.air-world.co.uk).
GETTING THERE Take the A487 from Caernarfon south towards Porthmadog for 4 miles, then the A499 towards Pwllheli for 7 miles, then take a sharp right into very a narrow lane at Gyrn Goch.
PUBLIC TRANSPORT There's a regular bus service (0871 2002233) less than ½ mile away to/ from Caernarfon, Porthmadog, Pwllheli and Nefyn (www.traveline-cymru.info).
OPEN Easter–end Oct.
IF IT'S FULL Other Cool Camping sites locally include Mynydd Mawr (p253), Treheli Farm (p249) and Tir Bach (p241).

Aberafon, Gyrn Goch, Caernarfon, Gwynedd, LL54 5PN		
t	01286 660295	w www.aberafon.co.uk	46 on the map

tir bach

Despite the fact that scenery is always made up of a limited number of fairly fixed features – water, rocks, grass, trees – the way they're arranged is infinitely variable, so no two places ever look exactly the same. But despite the fact that each place is unique, some places seem to be more unique than others.

The look of the landscape between the villages of Trefor, on the northern coast of the Llyn Peninsula and Porthdinllaen, about 10 miles south, is absolutely and totally unique. Nowhere else do such big, bleak, rocky mountains come plunging down so suddenly to the sea, yet manage to look so shapely. Nowhere else has fishing villages even remotely like Porth Nefyn and Porthdinllaen. And there's nowhere quite like the hidden valley of Nant Gwrtheyrn tucked away in the middle of the hills.

This relationship between steep hills and the shifting, shining waters washing around their feet is intoxicating stuff to those bitten deep by the scenic affliction and, once seen, this magical place draws you back.

Hidden in this huge dose of scenery, Nant Gwrtheyrn (just how is that pronounced?) used to be called Vortigern's Valley, as it was believed that the mythical giant lived in this

secluded Shangri-La. What has all this to do with camping, you may be wondering? Well, between the mountains of Yr Eifl in the north and those two idyllic fishing villages in the south, nestling on the cliffs, perches the small, retiring campsite of Tir Bach, totally surrounded by all this rampant uniqueness. But, huge though the surroundings are, the campsite is neither overawed nor intimidated and has a pleasant, open feeling about it.

This smallest of sites consists of just two modest-sized fields that slope gently towards the sea right next to the owners' house and provide everybody with a sea view and the maximum dose of sunshine during the long evenings of summer. Despite the sometimes harsh weather, Mr and Mrs Cartwright, who aren't Welsh but have been here long enough to qualify as honorary natives, always offer the warmest of welcomes and few campers come here without returning.

That pleasant and open feeling can seem a little bit exposed when nature gets herself into a bad mood, which happens frequently, so bring your storm gear to Tir Bach. However, the weather can change just as quickly for the better and the beaches of Nefyn, Porth Nefyn and Porthdinllaen then call, and with no vehicular access to

Porthdinllaen this is an especially tranquil and appealing cove. There's a pub by the edge of the water and, on a warm summer day, there can't be many better places to sit and sip while you watch the world go by.

The beaches lie about a mile from the site and it's a nice walk down to Nefyn along the Llyn Coastal Path, which at this point is actually inland, on the hill above the site. But if you like to pull your boots on to go exploring, the place to be is along the coast path to the north, several hundred metres above Porth y Nant, but below the immense hills that overlook the sea.

The very best of this scenic extravaganza can be found in Nant Gwrtheyrn, where abandoned quarries add a melancholic aura to the abundant natural beauty. Nestling on a shelf halfway down the valley is the Welsh Language Centre, housed in some of the former quarry buildings, with a situation such that to see the place may even inspire you to learn the language.

Scenery-wise, this is a startling – not to mention unique – area of Wales, and Tir Bach offers a basic but friendly place to soak it all up from.

THE UPSIDE Small peaceful site in brutally beautiful surroundings.
THE DOWNSIDE This stretch of coast catches all the weather it can possibly manage – and some of it isn't good.
THE DAMAGE £6 per night for a camping family. Dogs on leads are permitted.
THE FACILITIES The amenities are basic and could never be described as plush, but everything is well maintained and runs to toilets, showers, washbasins and a dishwashing sink. No hook-ups, but the only members of the motorhome family allowed are small campers.

NEAREST DECENT PUB There are several in the villages of Nefyn and Morfa Nefyn including the Dragon Bar within the Nanhoron Arms (01758 720203), where they serve a good range of food, but where the real attraction is the fact that this is the favoured haunt of the locals, whose language has a musical lilt to it. The Ty Coch (01758 720498) at Porthdinllaen must surely be one of the most appealingly situated pubs in the world.
IF IT RAINS All the attractions of Caernarfon are about 15 miles away, including the rather quaint Caernarfon Airworld Museum (01286 830800; www.air-world.co.uk) at Dinas Dinlle.

GETTING THERE Take the A487 from Caernarfon south, towards Porthmadog, for 4 miles, then the A499 towards Pwllheli, and on to the B4417 to Nefyn. The site is 5 miles along the B4417 on the right.
PUBLIC TRANSPORT There is a regular bus service from Caernarfon to Nefyn run by Traveline (08712 002233; www.traveline.org.uk); buses 14 and 27 stop about 500 metres down the road.
OPEN Whitsun–Sept.
IF IT'S FULL Other Cool Camping sites locally include Mynydd Mawr (p253) and Treheli Farm (p249).

Tir Bach, Pistyll, Nefyn, Pwllheli, Gwynedd LL53 6LW

| t | 01758 720074 | 47 on the map |

penrallt

It is rumoured that a famous Victorian philosopher, in one of his more lucid moments (assuming philosophers have them, that is), may have said 'All campsites are equal, but some are more equal than others', and this brings Penrallt Coastal Camping to mind. Not so much because it is more equal than others, but more because of the philosophy of social responsibility that underpins the everyday ethos of the place. Yeah, yeah, I know it all sounds a bit serious for describing a campsite, which, after all, is just a place you go for your holidays and a bit of fun, but Penrallt definitely proves that fun, holidays and good ecological awareness make comfy bedfellows.

Where to start? The owners, Pete and Sue, arrived here a few years ago fully aware of what a magical spot this is in ecological terms and were desperate to keep it that way. Folk have been camping here for generations, but the quandary they faced was how to carry on camping while minimising the impact tourism inevitably inflicts on the environment. This is why they've installed reed beds for getting rid of unmentionable stuff, and why the recycling facilities are as comprehensive as they are obvious. The site motto is 'Striving for Sustainability' and for their efforts Pete and Sue have received a glorious Green Dragon Award.

But first and foremost Penrallt is a family campsite, ideal for those with young children who want to spend time with them and have them get involved with other children, rather than just seek out ready-made entertainment. The children's 'play' facilities here consist of bits and pieces such as an old boat, swings and even a tree that youngsters are allowed to climb. Encouraged even. The difficulty with telling the world that a campsite is perfect for young families is that it may deter others from coming, but it shouldn't, as the campers here are a happy mix of families and couples.

If you enjoy coastal walking, the stretch of coast alongside Penrallt has a well-marked scenic path for miles: one direction leads to the small harbour at Porth Ysgaden (just over a mile) and just beyond is the lovely little beach at Porth Towyn. Along the way the seals lounge around on the rocks, giving the wild-looking humans the once-over. In the opposite direction the cliffs relent about a mile from Penrallt on to the mile of empty golden sands at Traeth Penllech, which is perfect bucket-and-spade territory for young campers when the sun shines. Older youngsters can swim, snorkel the days away or try the surfing. Further afield there are hidden coves along the edge of this little-known extremity of Wales, and where

P&Q is assured. Talking of peace and quiet, outside school holidays, apparently, this is a secluded paradise for those who want to explore the far reaches of the peninsula and see its wildlife.

In the end this site is all about the place itself – the coast of the Llyn Peninsula and that sense of caring for the environment and its wildlife. This message is gently instilled, with colourful recycling bins and information about the wildlife, and all especially aimed at the children – the ones left to carry the can if we get it wrong.

This isn't just talk at Penrallt, though, for every September a weekend is set aside for a mass coastal clean-up, when campsite fees are donated to the Marine Conservation Society in exchange for campers helping rid the Llyn's coast of damaging rubbish and pollution, which arrives with each new tide.

So are all campsites equal then? Well yes, but some are more equal than others, and this is certainly one of them.

THE UPSIDE Perfect for children, with room to play and loads of other kids onsite in school holidays. Beautiful location next to the sea towards the end of the Llyn Peninsula.
THE DOWNSIDE If the weather turns nasty there isn't a lot on offer to do locally, or even not-so locally. Take plenty of non-electronic games. Remember those?
THE DAMAGE Tent and 2 adults £10, additional adults £4, children £2, electric hook-ups £2, dogs £1, showers 20p.
THE FACILITIES Eccentric, quirky and slightly home-made would be the best way to describe the facilities. Recycled even. They are more than adequate, with toilets, family shower rooms, refrigerators for hire, laundry with large-capacity cold-water washing machine and dishwashing.

NEAREST DECENT PUB Only one and that's the Lion Inn in Tudweiliog (01758 770244). It has a decent menu and serves locally brewed ale from the Porthmadog Brewery, including the famous Purple Moose Bitter
IF IT RAINS The best advice is to arrange for dry weather during your stay (see 'the Downside'). However, all is not totally lost, as trendy Abersoch, with its bars and coffee bars, is about 12 miles away and if it's wet why not get even wetter – at Porth Neigwl, where the surfing can be quite exciting. With wetsuits the rain doesn't matter. Canoes can be launched and used safely at nearby Porth Ysgaden. It is also rumoured that there is a tea house in lovely little Aberdaron.
GETTING THERE Set your sat-nav and hope it knows what it's doing. Failing that, follow the A487

south from Caernarfon for 3 miles, then the A499 south for 10 miles, the B4417 south-west for 12 miles and half a mile beyond Tudweiliog turn right into a lane, then keep left until you see campsite signs. Good luck.
PUBLIC TRANSPORT There's a regular bus service to and from Pwllheli.
OPEN Easter–end Oct.
IF IT'S FULL Other local *Cool Camping* sites include Mynydd Mawr (p253), Treheli Farm (p249), Tir Bach (p241) and Aberafon (p237).

Penrallt Coastal Camping, Tudweiliog, Pwllheli, Gwynedd LL53 8PB

| t | 01758 770654 | w | www.penrallt.co.uk | 48 | on the map |

treheli farm

Treheli Farm is another of those places where you bring your tent for something other than simply somewhere to bring your tent.

While it's true that Treheli is just another holiday destination in the great scheme of things, this is more of a place to say 'goodbye cruel world' and offer yourself into a better one. But don't expect this better world to come fully equipped with all the latest mod-cons, because it doesn't. In fact, in an ablutionary sense, facilities here belong to another, far less better, world.

But the whole point about Treheli is the great location; it's perched delicately on a level ledge of ground elevated several hundred metres above the sea, with a spectacular view out over the beach of Porth Neigwl (Hell's Mouth).

This four-mile-long stretch of sand and its deeply soothing turquoise water must surely count as one of the most impressive beaches in Britain and, what's more, it's usually just as impressively empty. You could almost think that there's enough room for the whole of humanity to spend a day on the beach here and it still wouldn't be packed. This says something about the nature of Porth Neigwl, where there are never more than a couple of dozen people.

This small, quiet site overlooks the whole length of the beach and every pitch has the same wonderful view out across the sands and sea. The quiet, peaceful atmosphere on this site reflects perfectly the tranquillity of the view and the lack of urgency that surrounds life in the western extremities of the Llyn Peninsula.

It's a short stroll down to the deserted sands from the site (though a little more huff and puff may be required on the return leg), or the fortunate few who camp here can stroll off in other more hilly directions on to Mynydd Rhiw. Paths seem to be everywhere and several lead to the small-but-perfectly-formed stately home of Plas-y-Rhiw, on the rocky flanks of the mini-mountain.

The beach at Porth Neigwl is best known for its truly delinquent surfing conditions but, generally speaking, the site is sheltered from the south-westerlies that pile the waves up so high in the bay below. Three southerly miles along the coastal path, the feet fall upon the scenic joys of Porth Ysgo and in another three miles the small seaside village of Aberdaron lies waiting to be discovered.

In the other direction from Treheli, after the beach, a further four miles of strolling brings the resort of Abersoch into view. This is where the 30-somethings from the Cheshire stockbroker belt take their leisure and where the raft of decent restaurants reflect this.

It seems a shame to ever get back in a car again after a few days of unwinding the motoring tensions at Treheli, but the roads on the western side of the Llyn are very quiet and all lead to places that deserve to be anything but peaceful. The western fringe of the peninsula hides a succession of beautiful little coves that rarely get busy, even in the mayhem of midsummer. Porth

Oer is the most popular and easiest to get at, while Porth Iago and Traeth Penllech are achingly good-looking.

There are days out aplenty to be had from Treheli if the urge takes you, including the ancient charms of Caernarfon and Criccieth, where there is also a castle and perhaps the best ice cream shop in the world. But wherever you wander on the lovely Llyn there will be nowhere lovelier than the view from your own tent, and no better life than that of a beach bum with a Treheli address.

THE UPSIDE Spectacular location overlooking Porth Neigwl.
THE DOWNSIDE Antiquated facilities and quite remote if you're a social animal.
THE DAMAGE Pitch (including 2 adults) £15 per night. Camper vans £20 per night. Furry friends welcome, too.
THE FACILITIES In a word, rubbish. There are toilets, showers and washbasins at the farmhouse over the road, but they're criminally neglected and antiquated. No other facilities and the nearest shop

isn't for miles. Bring everything you need.
NEAREST DECENT PUB The Sun Inn at Llanengan (01758 712660), 4 miles away, is a good, traditional pub with a decent restaurant, or at the other end of the spectrum, the Fresh Café Bar and Grill (01758 710033; www.freshabersoch. co.uk) in Abersoch is a lively place with a reasonable selection of good-value dishes, plus a cocktail menu. There are also several excellent restaurants on the High Street in Abersoch.
IF IT RAINS Take some good books or your

wetsuit. Or there are always the pubs in Abersoch.
GETTING THERE Take the A499 from Pwllheli towards Abersoch. At Abersoch, take the road signposted to Llangian, then follow the lane towards Rhiw. Treheli is on the old coast road.
PUBLIC TRANSPORT Buses 17b and 31 stop nearby.
OPEN May–Oct.
IF IT'S FULL Mynydd Mawr (p253) is nearby, or try Rhydolion (01758 712342; www.rhydolion. co.uk) at Llanengan, Porth Neigwl.

Treheli Farm, Treheli, Rhiw, Pwllheli, Gwynedd LL53 8AA

| | | t | 01758 780281 | 49 | on the map |

mynydd mawr

It almost seems as though Mynydd Mawr lies on the very edge of the known world, at the far western tip of the Llyn Peninsula. In glorious isolation, it's sheltered from the prevailing winds, but has a stunning view out across to Bardsey Island. Once upon a time, the island was an important pilgrimage destination and it was thought that a quick trip across the water to it could possibly save your soul.

They obviously knew a thing or two back then, because in our busy world, a camping pilgrimage to Mynydd Mawr could very well do the same job. This out-of-the-way place rarely gets crowded; the site is small, the rugged scenery is massive and there is an overwhelming feeling of being hugged by Mother Nature – now there's a thought.

One of the most noticeable things about this place is the silence or, possibly more accurately, the lack of noise. Of course you can hear the sea, the birds and the wind, but the lack of cars, aeroplanes and boats, even, has the unusual effect of an obvious – but welcome – silence. Listening to the silence may seem like an odd thing to do, but you just can't help yourself here.

If late-evening strolls are your thing, then Mynydd Mawr is the place to take them. The walk from the campsite to the westernmost extremity of the Llyn, to watch the sun plunge into the red western sky, is one of life's finest privileges.

Anyway, enough of this delightfully dreamy contemplation – there is a lengthy inventory of scenery out there awaiting campers' inspection. The Llyn Peninsula Coastal Path passes the site (it couldn't really avoid it) and offers you the opportunity to stride off along the edge of the world to Aberdaron in one direction or to Porth Oer in the other.

Aberdaron has a café or two, a pub, a nice beach, a quaint little church and the chance to get on a boat to visit Bardsey Island. To call Aberdaron a resort would be ludicrous, but after the isolation of Mynydd Mawr, it feels almost like re-entry into the world. You can even buy an ice cream there and rent a chair on the beach, though any plans for a theme park are a long way off. The walk to Porth Oer along the northern and western fringe is among a much bigger and wilder landscape, with 240-metre cliffs plunging into the restless waters, while Porth Oer, about four very rough miles away, is a soft, inviting place of golden sands.

The Llyn Peninsula isn't the kind of place to go if you're seeking bright lights and entertainment and Mynydd Mawr lies at the very bottom of this scenic cul-de-sac, so getting elsewhere will never be achieved quickly on the narrow, bumpy roads. But there are other places that warrant a good look: Porth Ysgo, about five miles east, is a scenic cove, where there's a fair chance that you'll have the beach to yourself, while a few more miles further east is the enormous beach at Porth Neigwl (p249), or Hell's Mouth, as it's known by the English.

It can seem like heaven on a sunny summer's day, but when the westerlies whip up the water into a bad temper, the name seems a little more apt and it's then that the surfing set take to the water.

But wherever you venture on the lovely Llyn, to return to Mynydd Mawr for that sunset stroll – and to listen again to that sound of silence – it's a haunting experience.

THE UPSIDE Total peace and quiet at the very tip of the Llyn Peninsula.
THE DOWNSIDE See 'If It Rains'.
THE DAMAGE Tent and 2 adults from £8 per night. Dogs are permitted if they are on leads.
THE FACILITIES Basic, but clean, with toilets, showers, dishwashing and a few electric hook-ups.
NEAREST DECENT PUB The Ship Inn (01758 760204), 2 miles away at Aberdaron, serves outstanding food in an intimate, wall-to-wall-carpeted, front-room-style setting.

Additionally, pubs, bars and eateries abound in Abersoch (p250).
IF IT RAINS Pray it doesn't – this is a good-weather destination, and there ain't much on offer if it turns wet. The nearest place to take shelter is at Abersoch (see above), some 14 miles distant. It's the social epicentre of the Llyn Peninsula, with its bars, restaurants and coffee shops.
GETTING THERE From the north, take the M56, then the A55 to Caernarfon. Follow the A487 towards Porthmadog for 3 miles, then turn

right on to the A499 to Llanbedrog. At Abersoch, take the B4413 to Aberdaron, then follow signs for Uwchmynydd. The site is a further mile past the chapel.
OPEN Mar–Oct.
IF IT'S FULL Another good campsite in the area is Ty-Newydd (01758 760581) half a mile before Mynydd Mawr, which also offers great views of Bardsey Island.

Mynydd Mawr, Llanllawen Fawr, Aberdaron, Pwllheli, Gwynedd LL53 8BY

| | t | 01758 760223 | w | www.aberdaroncaravanandcampingsite.co.uk | 50 | on the map |

acknowledgements

Cool Camping: Wales (2nd edition)
Series Concept and Series Editor: Jonathan Knight
Researched, written and photographed by:
Jonathan Knight, Sophie Dawson, Keith Didcock,
Sam Pow and Andy Stothert
Project Manager: Sophie Dawson
Produced by Bookworx (Editorial: Jo Godfrey Wood
Design: Peggy Sadler)
Cover Design: Kenny Grant
Proofreaders: Nikki Sims, Leanne Bryan
Publishing Assistant: Cassidie Alder
Marketing: Shelley Bowdler
PR: Carol Farley

Published by: Punk Publishing, 3 The Yard,
Pegasus Place, London SE11 5SD

Distributed by: Portfolio Books, 2nd Floor, Westminster
House, Kew Road, Richmond, Surrey TW9 2ND

All photographs © Jonathan Knight/Sophie Dawson/
Keith Didcock/Sam Pow/Andy Stothert/Shellani Gupta/
Sue Smith, except the following (all reproduced with
permission); p146 © Reuters/Russell Boyce;
p148 top © Big Pit: National Coal Museum, Blaenafon/
Amgueddfu Cymru – National Museum of Wales;
bottom © National Roman Legion Museum, Caerleon/
Amgueddfu Cymru – National Museum of Wales; p149
top © National Slate Museum, Llanberis/Amgueddfu
Cymru – National Museum of Wales; bottom © St
Fagans: National History Museum, Cardiff/Amgueddfu
Cymru – National Museum of Wales; p216 © Green
Man/Shot2Bits; p218 top © Green Man/Shot2Bits;
bottom © Abergavenny Food Festival/Nathan Morgan;

p219 top © Wakestock/Sim Bradley (Alliance).
Front cover: Cae Du © Andy Stothert.

Many of the photographs featured in this book are
available for licensing. For more information, see
www.coolcamping.co.uk.

The publishers and authors have done their best
to ensure the accuracy of all information in *Cool
Camping: Wales*, however, they can accept no
responsibility for any injury, loss or inconvenience
sustained by anyone as a result of information
contained in this book.

Punk Publishing takes its environmental
responsibilities seriously. This book has been
printed on paper made from renewable sources and
we continue to work with our printers to reduce our
overall environmental impact. Wherever possible,
we recycle, eat organic food and always turn the
tap off when brushing our teeth.

A BIG THANK YOU! Thanks to everyone who has
written and emailed with feedback, comments and
suggestions. It's good to see so many people at one
with the *Cool Camping* ethos. In particular, thanks
to the following readers for telling us about their
favourite places to camp: Andy Brett, Sally Burgess,
Phil Colebrook, Simon Conlan, Louise Crockhart, Elgan
Daniel, Jane Hargrave, Iain Harper, Charlie Hemp,
Vicky Henry, Pam Jakeman, Kathie Jessup, Annie
Kippax and Rachel Morgan.

HAPPY CAMPERS?

We hope you've enjoyed reading *Cool Camping: Wales* and that it's inspired you to get out there.

The campsites featured in this book are a personal selection chosen by the *Cool Camping* team. None of the campsites has paid a fee for inclusion, nor was one requested, so you can be sure of an objective choice of sites and honest descriptions. We have visited hundreds of campsites across Wales to find this selection, and we hope you like them as much as we do. However, it hasn't been possible to visit every single Welsh campsite. So, if you know of a special place that you think should be included, we'd like to hear about it.

Send us an email telling us the name and location of the campsite, some contact details and why it's special. We'll credit all useful contributions in the next edition of the book, and senders of the best emails will receive a complimentary copy. Thanks and see you out there!

wales@coolcamping.co.uk